PERFECT
PALETTE

PERFECT PALETTES

Inspiring Colour Choices
for the Home Decorator

Stephanie Hoppen
text by Joanna Copestick

jacqui small

First published in 2010 by Jacqui Small LLP,
an imprint of Aurum Press Ltd
7 Greenland Street
London NW1 0ND

Text copyright © Jacqui Small LLP 2009
Photography, design and layout copyright © Jacqui Small LLP 2009

The author's moral rights have been asserted.

PUBLISHER Jacqui Small
EDITORIAL MANAGER Kerenza Swift
EDITOR Sian Parkhouse
ART DIRECTOR Sarah Rock
PRODUCTION Peter Colley

ISBN: 978 1 906417 31 4

2012 2011 2010
10 9 8 7 6 5 4 3 2 1
Printed in Singapore

CONTENTS

inspired by colour

I've always been excited about the ways in which colour can be employed to transform a space, whether it is in the form of pictures, wall paint or wallpaper, furniture or fabric.

The glorious thing about colour is the abundance of energy and emotion it brings to a space, whether a cappuccino-toned relaxing living room or a smart, enlivening burgundy-inspired dining space. From cool hues and pale off-whites to rich cyclamen pinks and life-enhancing leaf greens, this book is about making colour work, taking inspiration from key designers and their personal colour philosophy, and applying colour knowledge to every room in the home. Colour is making a come-back. The long love affair with everything pale and neutral is not over, but new tones of subtle colour are now being suffused with the old favourites to create clean, bright warming spaces.

Everyone has their own unique sense of colour derived from all kinds of sources. Favourite colours may be a result of well-remembered places or things from childhood, a special item of clothing or a treasured object, or a particular place such as a comfortable kitchen.

Often responses to the world around us are formed from perceived colours – the joy of a holiday seascape, the fascinating tonal variations

OPPOSITE Hilton McConnico's Paris apartment is a virtuoso study in cool eau-de-nil, complementary reds and analogous lilacs and purples, with a wall of mirror rather than a wall of colour that serves to reflect all the tones back into the space.

found in a forest in autumn or a perfect plate of complementary tomato and basil salad. These winning combinations can sometimes be transposed as colour schemes to rooms with great effect; others may need toning down to achieve a similarly pleasing emotional response.

Walking into a room where the colour is right is akin to enjoying a perfectly balanced meal or listening to uplifting music – a sensory delight, mood-enhancing and satisfying to linger in. Colour, elegantly handled, is as important as a carefully chosen piece of furniture or a well laid-out room in creating a home. It is a vital component in making a space feel alive and welcoming.

Designing with colour is all about choosing what feels right for you, choosing a palette you will want to live with. If your wardrobe is packed with blue clothes, the chances are you will also be drawn to blues and similar tones when it comes to decorating your home.

Getting colour right calls for some intuition, a few basic rules for combining colour and an understanding of how colours work, together and alone. This book explains the properties, performance and personality of different colours, shows how to look at colour and assess why it works, and provides dozens of palette choices and variations across the colour spectrum, from warm pink and active green to cool neutral oatmeal and seductive aubergine. Now go paint!

OPPOSITE TOP LEFT At the Hotelito in Baja, California, Jenny Armit has used punchy fuchsia and vivid denim walls as highlights on an exterior that is painted heavenly blue to blend in with the constant sun. These colours are so at home here, where they look bright but not brash.

OPPOSITE TOP RIGHT Broken colour in neutral tones makes for smart sophistication, indoors or out, in this Moroccan hideaway designed by Karl Fournier and Olivier Marty of Studio KO. Earthy tones team well with natural basketweave furniture and a polished concrete floor.

OPPOSITE BOTTOM LEFT Soft lilacs, blues and grey whites are both subtle and pretty in Lena Proudlock's country kitchen, where the palette is based on pale parma violet and summery tones.

OPPOSITE BOTTOM RIGHT In a scrupulously simple room designed by Ulla Hagar Tornos, where wood is the dominant feature, a subtle and contemplative palette of cool greys in varying tones used on walls and woodwork creates a harmonious colour story that works as well for an East Coast setting as it would in northern Europe.

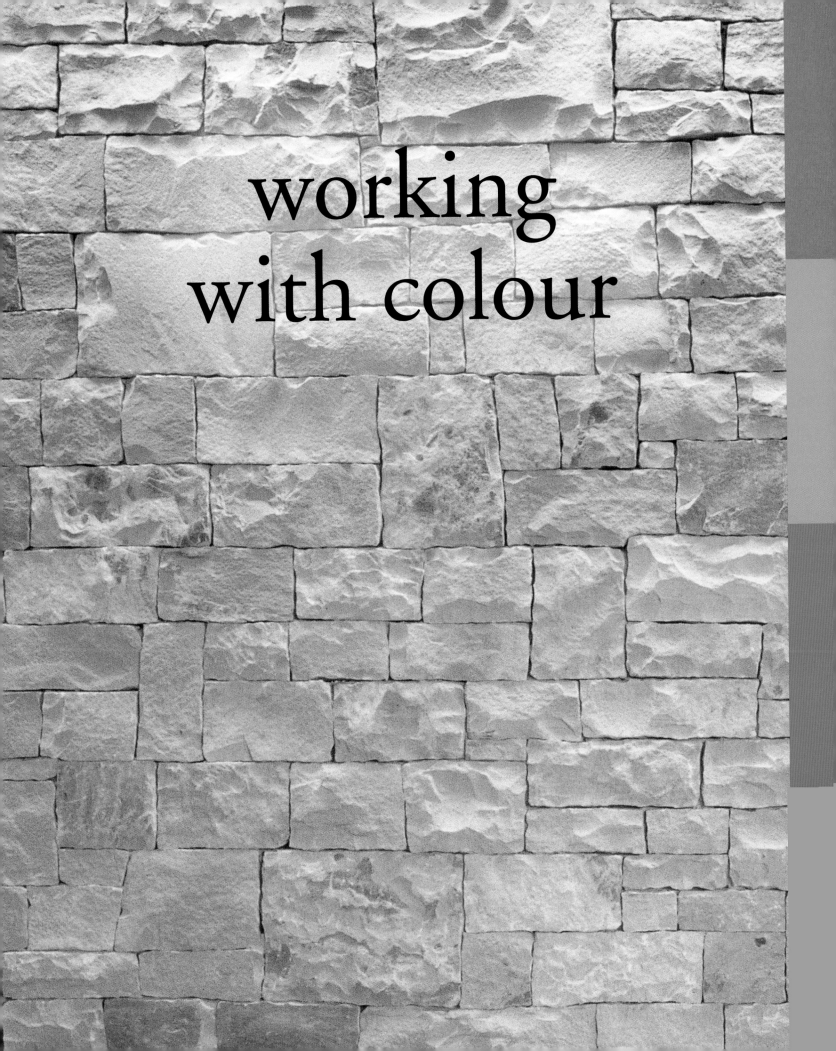

working
with colour

GETTING COLOUR RIGHT

ABOVE New York-based designer Jamie Drake has created layers of mellow yellow for this bedroom in which animal print furnishings are right at home against walls that evoke a hot African sun.

RIGHT Soft broken colour applied in a wash to the walls provides ample texture in a light and airy bedroom, designed by Karl Fournier and Olivier Marty of Studio KO. The only additional colour needed is added in the curtains, in the form of deep purple, to emphasize the subtle pink pigment on the walls.

COLOUR IS A VITAL TOOL FOR CREATING SUCCESSFUL INTERIORS, AND WHETHER IT IS USED IN STRONG TONES OF GENEROUS PROPORTIONS OR AS A SUBTLE BACKDROP TO SMALLER JOLTS OF COLOUR, IT IS VERY OFTEN THE COLOUR THAT FIRST STRIKES YOU ON ENTERING A ROOM.

The new colours that excite me are the interesting, muted but elegant tones that bring warmth and energy to a space. Shades such as steely hibiscus blues, muted French greys, ultra-chic celery and delicate alabaster. And there are strong tones too, such as full-on fuchsia, rich, deep aubergine and dark, dramatic periwinkle. Plus, of course, the perfect white – pannacotta if you will – which is not white at all, but rather a mix of white with hints of other hues to 'dirty' it up and create the impression of a neutral backdrop.

These inspiring colours are all around us, in nature, food, art and architecture, from Rajasthan to Reykjavik, Florida to Florence. They are a mix of the contemporary and the comfortable, understated but inspiring, delicate but not elusive, strong but not overpowering. Colour is one of life's great luxuries, it is inspiring to work with and extremely satisfying to live with when you get it right. Creating palettes of harmonious tones or complementary shades is an uplifting and invigorating process, just the ticket for re-energizing interiors and creating a whole new atmosphere for a room.

The application of scientific theory to choosing colours for the home has some value, but it should not dictate hard and fast rules when it comes to choosing perfect palettes. Colour wheels and colour saturation charts can confound more than inspire; I find I work with colour on an instinctive basis. It is of course useful and necessary to have an awareness of which colours work naturally with or complement one another, but often it is how a colour makes you feel that will be a starting point in a room. We've all seen colour mistakes, where all-pervasive shades that jar the senses have been misguidedly seen as 'taking a bold approach', or where the dreaded magnolia has been solely employed as a 'safe' option.

It has been inspiring talking to some of the most inventive paint makers and designers around to find out why they make and use the paint they do. Francesca Wezel of Francesca's Paints draws her inspiration from years of travel to exotic locations, while David Oliver of The Paint Library takes an almost scholarly approach to selecting and refining a unique palette of perfect off-whites. In New York Jamie Drake is unique in his use of vivid colours, from sunshine yellow to primary pink, and French designer Agnès Emery employs a range of rich blues, greens and yellows in her colourful interiors that are full of multi-coloured tiles and saturated colours.

Those designers noted for their innate sense of colour, such as Tara Bernard, often go beyond the confines of pure colour theory, mixing and matching tones and hues of the same colour band as much as they do distinct colours.

TOP LEFT A nautical country palette in a Cornish dining room calls for the traditional creamware combination of powder blue and clotted cream for its seaside inspiration.

TOP RIGHT Pink can work as a wall colour if it is kept towards the red or salmon end of the spectrum so it doesn't stray into baby pink territory.

BOTTOM LEFT This glorious light-filled coastal home by Jane Churchill is a white-on-white story offset by lime-coloured cushions, deep green topiary and delicate off-white upholstery. Simply charming.

BOTTOM RIGHT Various shades of green are a good substitute for a treescape in this children's room in a midtown urban apartment in New York. Green often works best when used in a combination of shades rather than as a blanket approach.

HOW COLOUR WORKS

'Colour is the most simple and obvious defining element in the personality of a place. It can subtly alter one's mood, so it should therefore be handled carefully, but that does not mean timidly. Call upon your own deepest instincts for inspiration.'

AGNÈS EMERY, EMERY & CIE

THE COLOUR WHEEL WAS FIRST DEVISED BY THE SCIENTIST ISAAC NEWTON WHO DISCOVERED THAT WHITE LIGHT SPLITS INTO THE COLOURS OF THE SPECTRUM WHEN SHONE THROUGH A PRISM. WHEN HE REFRACTED LIGHT THIS WAY, A RAINBOW OF SEVEN COLOURS BECAME VISIBLE – RED, ORANGE, YELLOW, GREEN, CYAN (LIGHT BLUE), INDIGO (DARK BLUE) AND VIOLET. IT IS THESE SHADES THAT MAKE UP THE COLOUR WHEEL.

White light is really a combination of the three primary colours of red, blue and yellow. Combinations of these three colours then go to make up the secondary colours of purple, orange and green. Tertiary colours are those that appear on the wheel between these primary and secondary colours, and are a result of mixing primary and secondary hues together: red-orange, yellow-orange, yellow-green, blue-green, blue-violet and red-violet.

Complementary colours are those that sit opposite one another on the colour wheel: blue and orange; red and green; violet and yellow are all complementary. They bring out the vivid tones in each other's hues, creating strong contrasts. Harmonious colours are those that sit next to one another on the wheel and work well together, such as tones of yellow through to terracotta, or aubergine to violet.

Using colours according to their natural associations on the colour wheel can be a bright and vivid exercise in colour combining if you choose the darker shades on the spectrum. But equally, if you use subtler shades of the main colours, and their many associated tones, a more gentle picture emerges that can be just as satisfying.

COLOUR AND LIGHT

The texture of paint itself will make a difference to how a colour is perceived (see Paints and Finishes, pages 18–19) and this is because of the way it reflects natural light. Matt and chalky paints such as those made by Francesca's Paints, Farrow & Ball and Fine Paints of Europe give depth to a room, thereby making it seem bigger. Shiny, glossy paints and finishes such as silk emulsions on walls and eggshell on woodwork tend to make a room look smaller, because they reflect the light back rather than absorbing it. This process is the same for both light and dark colours.

The reason why trying to reproduce Rajasthan pink on a bedroom wall in Ireland or a muted Swedish oxblood red in a Mediterranean hacienda will create a paint mistake is also the effect of natural light. To create the desired effect you would have to choose 'muddied' tones of a similar colour in the northern hemisphere or use the same colour ramped up to a vivid tone where the sun shines brightly.

Where natural light is limited, it is actually a good idea to use colour. Brilliant white used in the northern hemisphere actually produces an ugly grey effect, especially when artificial light is thrown on it. It is far better to use off-whites mixed with yellow ochre, raw umber or burnt umber toned pigments to soften the effect. Francesca Wezel says: 'After 20 years of working with colours, the shades that work best in the northern hemisphere are off-whites, fawns, taupes, yellows and terracottas.' Even within the northern hemisphere, the natural light is different in Scandinavia than it is in mainland Europe. In the Nordic countries blue works better when it is mixed with grey tones, altogether more faded than the knocked-back tones of blue mixed with beige that would work in London, Paris or Amsterdam.

GETTING THE WHITE RIGHT

Too often home decorators, faced with an array of off-white tins of paint and colour charts, will opt for the shade they have heard of. Magnolia has a lot to answer for. It's not even on the pure spectrum, either in paint terms or in colour terms. Its poor reputation these days stems from an over-use of it during the 1980s and 1990s as a poor-quality, vinyl-based trade paint that was tinted with a little too many pink tones. It was deemed uncontroversial, a safe bet. Nowadays, thankfully, there are myriad shades of elegant off-white and neutrals that are worth exploring as a base colour for rooms.

Paint technology, like everything else in our lives, is changing. A more planet-friendly approach to paint ingredients and manufacturing processes has meant a more eco-friendly attitude. Francesca's Paints in London has championed some truly amazing limewash and eco-emulsion paints. In her Battersea headquarters, Francesca Wezel performs amazing paint alchemy to produce natural paints using limewash, natural pigments and other eco-friendly raw materials to create stunning colours that are at the couture end of the decorator's toolbox. She is an acknowledged expert in paints and palettes, which range from almost translucent off-white shades of alabaster and white truffle to stronger tones inspired by a sense of place.

ROOM FOR COLOUR

OPPOSITE TOP LEFT In Hilton McConnico's Paris house turquoise green and acid yellow combine to make a tart but smart palette, especially when outlined with black detailing on furniture, curtains and accessories. This is unusual but uplifting.

OPPOSITE TOP RIGHT In Jamie Drake's New York apartment one of his signature colours, a simply splendid powder pink, provides both decoration and visual interest in a pared-down space.

OPPOSITE BOTTOM LEFT Kitchen designer Johnny Grey is renowned for his sense of colour and for mixing materials and shapes This combination of steel, marble, bubblegum pink and cornflower blue provides hints of Mexico.

OPPOSITE BOTTOM RIGHT Dark chocolate walls are brought to life with plump yellow cushions and ceramics in a room that is traditional, but with a colourful twist.

ABOVE RIGHT Seaside artefacts and framed textiles set against walls the colour of cloudless skies create the perfect nautical palette of red, white and blue.

IF A WHOLE ROOM CONJURES A COMPLETE PICTURE, THEN THE WALLS SHOULD BE THE BLANK CANVAS STARTING POINT. INSPIRATION MAY TAKE THE FORM OF A KEY PIECE OF FURNITURE OR THE UPHOLSTERY, THE LEVEL OF NATURAL LIGHT, OR AN ARCHITECTURAL FOCAL POINT SUCH AS A FIREPLACE OR A HIGH, ORNATE CEILING.

Colour is a personal thing, but it is good to bear in mind the general principles before you start playing with colour. Restraint, rather than rampant adventures with pigment, often produces the best results. If you want to create a strong, sure sense of colour, one approach advocated by designers is to avoid lurid planes of saturated shades on all four walls in favour of well-placed accents around the room. This could take the form of a single wall in a robust shade, or brightly coloured accessories such as curtains, throws, cushions and lamps used to provide punctuated points of colour in the room.

Establishing a mix of tone, texture and scale in a range of harmonious shades to create a welcoming whole, is often the most successful way of creating a cohesive scheme. Using paint on wooden panelling, woodwork and floors is important, too, if you wish to tie together all the elements in a space.

Paint will often look darker when used over a large area of wall, so when choosing paint colours, select paint samples that are a couple of shades lighter than your perceived finished colour. Play around with shades and colours before you commit them to walls. It's best to experiment by painting on a taster patch of colour before buying all your paint, as often the colour you have in your head may be different from what is actually in the can.

LOOK AT THE SPACE

Colour can be used as a tool to contract or enlarge a space, create a cosy atmosphere, disguise awkward architectural features and enhance or diminish natural light.

Darker colours such as rich burgundies, stormy blues and heritage greens will visually bring the walls together and make a room feel smaller and more intimate, while whites and off-whites will create airy surroundings, allowing light to filter onto all surfaces.

Some colours have a natural affinity for certain spaces, such as blues, greens and whites in bathrooms, where water and mirrors reflect and refract the colours, creating the sense of a micro-seascape indoors. In kitchens where wooden cupboards and surfaces abound, pale neutrals work as good companions to mid-tone woods such as oak and beech, while glossy, sleek contemporary units in black, white or lacquer red all benefit from white or off-white walls, so the units can do the colour-talking.

PAINTED FLOORS

Painted floors are so very á la mode and a great way of completing a palette in a room, both anchoring a scheme and providing a rich surface underfoot for colours to work with. For a sleek finish it's best to use gloss or eggshell paint, which provides a pleasing patina and is tough and durable for foot traffic. To create a vintage look, dilute the paint with white spirit. Brush on the paint, then remove the top layer with muslin to distress the surface.

'If I am feeling neutral it is linen white, as it goes with everything. But really it depends, as every room is different: it depends on the architecture, the light coming in though the window, what way the windows face, and if there are any obstructions outside. All these make a difference.' KIT KEMP, HOTEL DESIGNER

PAINTS AND FINISHES

COLOUR WILL PERFORM IN DIFFERENT WAYS ACCORDING TO HOW IT IS APPLIED TO WALLS AND FLOORS. MATT SURFACES GIVE DEPTH TO A ROOM AND MAKE IT APPEAR LARGER, WHILE GLOSS SURFACES REFLECT LIGHT AROUND RATHER THAN ABSORB IT. IN DARK SPACES IT IS BEST TO USE SOME FORM OF COLOUR RATHER THAN BRILLIANT WHITE OR GREY, WHICH WILL EMPHASIZE A LACK OF LIGHT.

When thinking about which type of paint to use, consider the size of your room, the amount of natural light it receives and whether you want the atmosphere to be one of relaxation or activity, and the use formal or informal.

Matt Emulsion paint is water-based, easy to apply and quick to dry. It normally has a low VOC rating (volatile organic compound), which means it is kinder to the environment than harsh gloss paints. While it is wipeable it may not be washable. It can be diluted with water to lighten its shade. Suitable for interior plaster walls, lining paper and ceilings.

Vinyl Silk or Satin Emulsion is tougher and more durable than matt emulsion and has a mid-sheen finish. It is washable and so suitable for walls that experience high traffic such as halls, stairways and landings.

Gloss is an oil-based paint that is tough, shiny and less environmentally friendly than emulsion paint. Its ultra-sleek sheen finish works well on woodwork, furniture, floors and metal. It is sometimes used for walls and ceilings, too, in more daring schemes. Apply a primer undercoat first.

Eggshell is the oil-based equivalent of vinyl satin and gives a mid-range sheen for woodwork. It is also known as satinwood or semi-gloss and doesn't need an undercoat.

Water-based Eggshell is a more environmentally friendly version of eggshell, with a low sheen and low VOC rating.

Limewash is a traditional paint finish that allows a wall to breathe. It is particularly suitable for bare plaster walls, cement render or skimmed, unfilled walls where some natural moisture is present, such as stone farmhouses. It is not suitable for use on wood, or any non-porous surface, but can be used on top of lining paper if it is applied over a base coat of matt emulsion. It is available in interior and exterior versions. Always apply it using a brush rather than a roller. It produces an opaque, textured velvety look.

Eco Emulsion is a new type of zero-VOC content paint with an ultra-matt finish and low odour that is gaining popularity. Several paint producers are creating an ever-widening range of palettes, including Auro Organics, Nutshell Natural Paints, Ecolibrium and Eco Chic by Oliver Heath. It's suitable for use on walls.

Floor Paint is a low VOC-rated paint with an eggshell finish suitable for wooden and concrete floors. Produced by Farrow & Ball and Fired Earth, among others.

Varnishes are available in a variety of finishes, from dead flat to eggshell. Normally these days they have low VOC ratings and are used for protecting surfaces covered with water-based paint, whether for walls or for wood surfaces. Even varnishing very flat finishes will subtly alter the opacity of the surface so bear this mind when you are settling on a finish and final colour for your walls, and test out a small area before you commit yourself.

Wood Stain can be natural or coloured and is used on surfaces such as floors and furniture. It's best used on areas of low traffic as it wears less well than paint.

Kitchen and Bathroom Paint is devised especially for use in kitchens, bathrooms and basements. More moisture and mildew resistant than conventional paints, it is washable and available in satin or gloss finishes.

Metallic Paints often look like gold leaf but are also available in silver, copper and bronze as well as gold forms for applying to metal on top of an undercoat. New metallic wall paints have also been developed to provide a glamorous shimmer for living rooms and dining rooms. Craig & Rose produce a metallic-finish paint.

Glitter Paint is a topcoat glazed paint that dries clear and leaves a glint of glitter over any matt emulsion.

Buttermilk Paints These specialist traditional paints were once used to dull down the glossy surfaces of oil paintings, but are best known as the type of paint the Shakers used for their decorative painted woodwork. The non-reflective flat finish is prone to marking, but their natural ingredients make them a good choice for allergy sufferers.

sunshine & citrus

primrose
pampas
straw
hay bale
corn
honey
cheetah
stoneground
gilt
cornfield
barleytwist
desert sand
maize
soft clay
wheaten
parmigiana
maple syrup
citrus zest
summer sunshine
canary yellow
citron
monet yellow
cadmium yellow
provence
lemon drop
cape sunshine
toscana
tangerine
tangiers
gold
mango
pumpkin
marigold
butternut squash

ALL ABOUT YELLOW

Yellow is the colour of summer sunshine, upbeat and uplifting, not shy about shouting its presence. But every can of yellow paint should also perhaps come with a Caution: Handle with Care warning as it can be a tricky colour to get right.

Choosing a perfect yellow is not easy because its tone intensifies when painted on walls, more so than many other colours. While you may be seduced by the sunny shades on a tiny paint chip, the overall effect of even a single wall, or indeed a whole room of the same colour, can be overwhelming in reality.

The difficult child of the paint world, yellow is often unpredictable and can be quite contrary in a light-filled room. The glorious bright tones we associate with summer sun are often delicate to translate to northern hemisphere walls, such as New York apartments or an English town house, where light may not be in such abundant and regular supply.

As a general rule yellow is most at home in the natural light of the southern hemisphere, from Mexico to the Mediterranean and across to Africa and Australasia. This bright light has a more favourable effect on strong yellow than does cold northern light. Here, it's best to knock off any acid edges with warmer tones of soft gold or pale ochre, which are more sophisticated. Surface finish is important too. If a paint is very matt it will absorb more light and therefore make a space look larger.

David Oliver of The Paint Library in London says: 'Trying to translate the colour of Provençal sunflower fields to your kitchen walls can sometimes land you with a bad omelette shade, which is certainly not life enhancing. The answer is to experiment by painting a wooden box with a pale neutral undercoat, then applying coats of your chosen colour. It is important with strong shades to gain an impression of how they will bathe an entire room with the colour, and how they will change throughout the day according to light levels.'

Yellow is associated with sunny, uplifting emotions. But the precise shade of yellow that you carry in your mind's eye does not always translate to the paint tin or prepared wall – this is true of yellow more than any other colour – which is why your chosen colour can sometimes disappoint on the wall. To work in bright tones yellow ideally needs warm, sunny natural light to bring out its real colour values. The stronger tones are often best used as accents, such as ceramics, lighting or cushions, or in small areas within a room, say one wall or an alcove.

Across the Sunshine & Citrus palette yellow with a hint of black veers towards a muddy green, while red tones provide a warmth that will make it suitable for teaming with earthy rust colours and a wide variety of natural woods, from pale beech to deep mahogany.

Yellow's reputation as a fresh and lively sunny colour means it is often used in kitchens, where a sunny outlook, an atmosphere of bustling activity and a sense of purpose will be enhanced by this palette. It is said to stimulate the brain and promote a sense of open-mindedness and also aid concentration, so it also works well in larders, utility rooms and home offices, where transient activities or bursts of concentrated work take place.

Relaxing spaces such as living rooms, bedrooms and bathrooms do not usually gain much in ambience or restful atmosphere from being bathed in yellow, although paler shades may work nicely and become especially inviting when used in harmonizing or contrasting tones. Francesca Wezel of Francesca's Paints cites soft ochre yellow as one of her bestselling paint colours, alongside off-whites, fawns, taupe and terracotta.

Strong citric shades are best used in rooms suffused with generous amounts of warm natural light like that of the southern hemisphere.

PROVENCE

STONEGROUND

KEY LIME

'I have been using yellow more recently, in different ways and only in small and medium-scale rooms. When I want to surprise or provoke an emotional reaction I use yellow, because it affects your mood, transfers energy and promotes joy and happiness.'

ILARIA MIANI

MAIZE

GOLD

SAFFRON

USING YELLOW Yellow can be difficult to work with but it is rewarding when you get it right. While acid yellows can be cold unless they have red or brown elements in them, lemon yellow can create a warm and inviting palette, especially at the softer buttery yellow and ochre range of the spectrum. These are often the most successful shades to work with. Too often when trying to create a crisp citric tone it is easy to end up with a sickly acidic shade that calls for sunglasses rather than admiring glances, so exercise caution and restraint when working within this range.

Remember that any one colour, and especially yellow, can look completely different depending on the level of natural and artificial lighting in a space. If possible, paint large pieces of lining paper in your chosen colour and attach them temporarily to the walls you intend to paint. Check on them throughout the day and notice how they change colour according to the light levels. This is a particularly useful exercise if you are planning to paint an entire room in the same colour. Once you gain an impression of the true intensity of the colour at the times of day when you are likely to be using the room, you may decide to paint just one wall in the colour, or indeed to choose a different colour entirely.

Colourwashing, the technique of using several layers of watered-down paint, works very well for yellow as it is a colour that calls for subtlety, especially in a period house, where strong shades are best used as broken colour or as accents. If you are deliberately seeking to use uniform, bright tones then these are best suited to contemporary settings.

Yellow's complementary shade on the colour wheel is blue. While rich, deep yellow and blue is a classic and traditional palette for country kitchens, these two complementaries often work

Novices in yellow should stick to the softer ends of the sunshine spectrum for the best results.

best nowadays in subtle, muted combinations, with the yellow pushed towards a pale sand-like palette and the blue shifted to a muted blue-grey, almost Scandinavian in influence. Francesca Wezel of Francesca's Paints believes that blue and yellow together can look wrong if combined with one another in tones that are too strong. They also tend to look quite old fashioned.

Yellow also works well with greens and oranges, providing crisp uplifting palettes that are quite bold to the eye. Experiment with tangerine tones and pale primrose, or sunny yellows and deep leaf greens. This is not really a colour for using often on doors or woodwork in the strong tones. Although sandy ochre colours or faded primrose can work if teamed with pale grey walls, and a splash of yellow on a wooden fireplace surround could make a pleasing Scandinavian-style palette.

As an accent colour, strong imperial yellow works very well, but is most successful in rooms that benefit from plenty of strong light. You can get away much more easily with sherbet shades or jewel-bright tones by using them on small areas or as zingy punctuation points throughout a room on cushions, curtains or rugs.

For accenting yellow rooms, I particularly favour steely grey or black to provide both smart contrast and graphic definition for the space – this can be quite crisp but a sure statement. Use these defining tones to contain and enhance yellow on cushion piping, architectural elements such as skirting, doors and dados or on lamps and lampshades or furniture detailing.

OPPOSITE TOP LEFT Subtle tones of pale yellow ochre tinged with green make a sharp complement to mauve-blue details on furniture and in paintings. The palette is grounded with a smart slate grey floor.

OPPOSITE TOP RIGHT In this Los Angeles home a bitter lemon scheme has been applied to bookshelves and a wall, providing a vivid counterpoint to a big collection of art books, stimulating an enquiring mind perhaps.

OPPOSITE BOTTOM LEFT In urban England a buttercup yellow can only thrive in this kitchen/dining space due to massive amounts of natural light and an interesting monochrome pillar placed directly alongside the building.

OPPOSITE BOTTOM RIGHT In a hunting lodge in the Périgord region of France, rough plastered walls are colourwashed in pale tones of ochre and yellow layered on one another for a timeless feel.

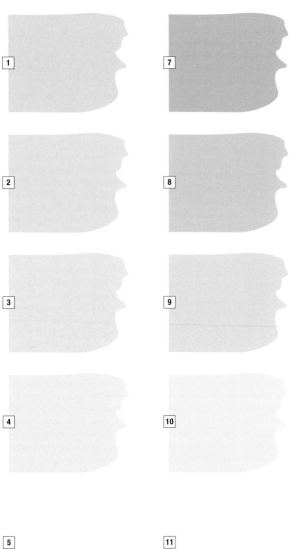

Yellows range from delicate primrose and enriching ochre shades to acid, uncompromising cadmium yellow. Experiment with muted tones to begin with as pure yellow can sometimes jar the senses.

ABOVE Ilaria Miani's Italian farmhouse kitchen combines clean lemon tones with a limed oak raftered ceiling and a stonework floor. Black detailing in the form of lampshades, suspended shelving and painted stripes on the table brings a smart finish and a slight contemporary twist to the space.

1 Cadmium Yellow

2 Provence

3 Citrus Zest

4 Sundance

5 Gilt Edge

6 Pale Primrose

7 Canary Yellow

8 Lemon Drop

9 Key Lime

10 Yellow Roses

11 Sunkissed

12 Butter Yellow

sunshine & citrus | sand

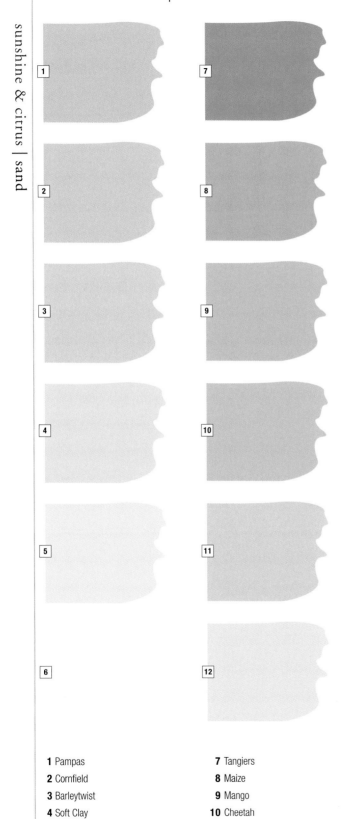

1 Pampas
2 Cornfield
3 Barleytwist
4 Soft Clay
5 Wheaten
6 Creamery

7 Tangiers
8 Maize
9 Mango
10 Cheetah
11 Desert Sand
12 Stoneground

sunshine & citrus | sunflower

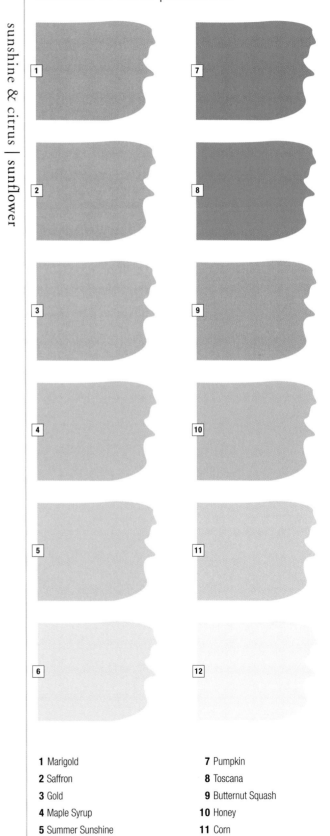

1 Marigold
2 Saffron
3 Gold
4 Maple Syrup
5 Summer Sunshine
6 Parmigiana

7 Pumpkin
8 Toscana
9 Butternut Squash
10 Honey
11 Corn
12 Buckwheat

'For each definite shade of yellow I would choose different references and matching colours that are in sympathy with them. Complementary tones for yellow in a traditional setting with antique, aged or mahogany furniture are shades of chestnut or maroon brown.' ILARIA MIANI

lemon

The lemon palette ranges from brilliant tones of sharp citrus at the vivid end of the spectrum to soft, understated pale primrose at the other. Citrus lemon is a crisp, lively colour that works particularly well in kitchens, where it is uplifting, friendly and outgoing. As a colour it is known to stimulate the mind, encouraging people to be alert, activating their memory and encouraging communication, so it is also a good choice for home offices or studies. For the same reasons it is less restful in a living room, although paler shades can certainly work well in relaxing spaces. Team lemon with crisp bright white, dark oaky brown or jet black for a sharp colour focus.

Very bright lemon, such as cadmium yellow or acid lemon-green, may irritate the nerves, so use these only as accents or on small areas at a time. Lemon is on the warm spectrum yet can often jolt the senses if it becomes too bright. Yellows with too much green will veer towards unflattering limey shades, especially under artificial light, so steer away from these if you are after a sharp lemon shade.

Traditional French Provençal houses often feature lemons of all tones as a signature colour, while imperial yellow was often seen in the smart Georgian houses of 19th-century London. Nowadays you are most likely to see lemon used in contemporary urban settings, often as statement walls in midtown lofts, or as accent pieces of furniture, such as chairs, in modern workplaces.

country retreat A Provençal

bedroom is pale, interesting and restful thanks to primrose walls and complementary powder blue bedding. Natural stonework, buttermilk-painted wood and a bleached brown floor tie the scheme together.

green accent Warm but muted, hazy walls

have been achieved by layering colourwashes one on another. An earth-toned floor and an elegant mahogany table work as counterpoints, allowing contrasting lapis green ceramics to take centre stage.

country retreat | above

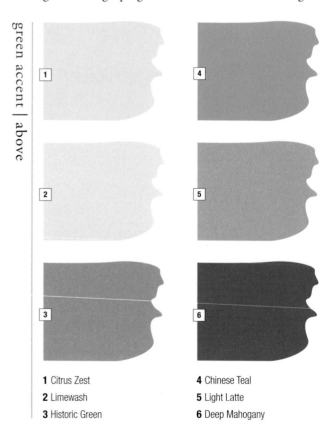

green accent | above

1 Sunkissed	4 Wedgwood Blue
2 White Truffle	5 Leather Chair
3 Cornflower Blue	6 Swedish Grey

1 Citrus Zest	4 Chinese Teal
2 Limewash	5 Light Latte
3 Historic Green	6 Deep Mahogany

breezy living A rich honey yellow infused

with reddish tones is perfectly combined with rust-red notes on the
blinds and in the soft furnishings. Neutral flooring fades into the
background to allow the reddish browns of a carved Indian cupboard
and a rattan coffee table to create a relaxed, welcoming atmosphere.

1 Sundance
2 White Truffle
3 Mystical Powers
4 Faded Grass
5 Mocha Magic
6 Red Brick Wall

'The first colour I ever made into a paint, called "Christophe's White", is the one that still sells the most. It combines three basic pigments, raw umber, burnt umber and yellow ochre – all warm shades. It is perfect for northern climes, as it takes away the greyness present in the natural light and warms up a space, without resorting to the dreaded "magnolia".' FRANCESCA WEZEL, FRANCESCA'S PAINTS

sand

Heading towards the soft yellow end of the spectrum, sandy colours include pale ochre tones where the yellow is dulled by a hint of brown as well as deeper wheat, stone and desert shades. These sandy shades are much more approachable and certainly more peaceful than lemon tones and are popular colours to work with, often forming the basis of an interesting neutral palette. They work well as part of an earthy palette, too, coupled with deep terracottas or warm cinnamon. And they can stand alone, providing calm, neutral backdrops on which you can layer accent colours from other palettes. For accent colours, add sunflower accessories in the form of tablecloths, artwork

or soft furnishings to sandy-coloured walls and you will impart a sense of 'sunshine by osmosis'. Or use harmonious tones of sandstone, beige or taupe for a multi-layered look that brings in other off-white or neutral tones.

Layers of texture also work well in sandy palettes, hinting at the desert and the seashore. Add this in the form of fabrics, rough ceramics or pottery, or even on the walls, by using rough plasterwork or applying specialist glazes or a colourwash, which give the flavour of a faded fresco wall. In at the deeper end, butternut squash and popcorn yellows with more of an orange bias are warming and inviting. Team them with browns and subtle taupes for a cohesive scheme that works as well in northern Europe as it does in warmer countries.

THIS PAGE A totally natural palette of pale sand and stone is a masterclass in using colours that are close to one another in a single palette, known as harmonious or analogous colours.

OPPOSITE Sandy ochre walls provide a pale but inviting backdrop for fabrics and upholstery in rich earthy shades.

cool provence

Simple French country architecture benefits from sand-coloured walls that enhance and define yellow-tinged, textured stonework. The space is elegant, with earthy accents in the flagstone floor and off-white furniture. Woodwork and accessories in a muted blue-grey echo the lavender-washed landscape.

cool provence | opposite

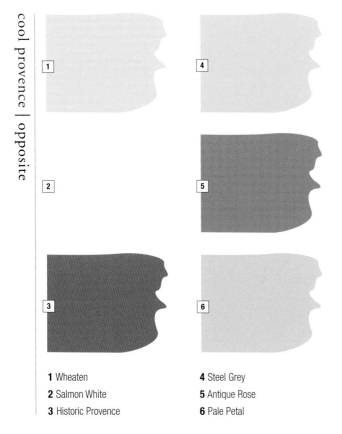

1 Wheaten

2 Salmon White

3 Historic Provence

4 Steel Grey

5 Antique Rose

6 Pale Petal

Perfect sand shades are those that include delicate traces of yellow, red or brown. Barely noticeable, these small tints provide a natural warmth, especially on unpapered plaster walls.

field of sand

This Pennsylvanian dining room takes its keynote tones of pale and deep yellows, complementary reds and greens and shades of orange from a folk art wall hanging. Rich sandy notes combine with apple red and deep green for a bold combination set against pale walls and an ochre-toned painted floor.

field of sand | above

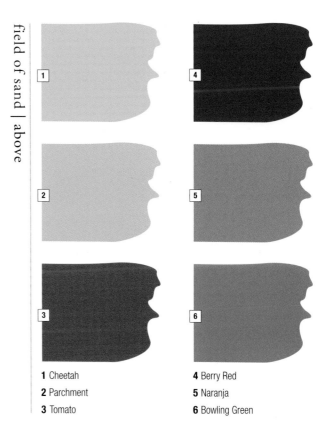

1 Cheetah

2 Parchment

3 Tomato

4 Berry Red

5 Naranja

6 Bowling Green

'Rooms that use colour lavishly are intriguing, intoxicating and inviting. The selection of a palette that you love is a sure-fire way to bring your personality home. Whether you opt for a multitude of vibrant accents to spark a more sedate surround, or you go for full-throttle colour everywhere, the introduction of colour guarantees a smashing interior.' JAMIE DRAKE

sunflower

The enriching tones of Provençal sunflower fields and the vivid ochre shades associated with Mexican haciendas are colours that are also capable of working in northern climes. They are at the warmer end of the sunshine spectrum, with a yellow ochre basis that includes enough orange in its make-up to survive under a cooler natural light and not give off a glow that is too greenish. These definite shades also work well as accent colours against leaf greens, opulent blues and deep reds; palettes in which deep base colours call for sharp counterpoints.

New York-based Jamie Drake is one of a few designers who embraces bright colour. He possesses an innate skill for infusing rooms with vivid tones that simply sing in a space, providing instant uplift and a vibrant atmosphere. He often combines such colours with bold and eclectic pieces of furniture to really bring a room to life.

Elsewhere, in Mexico, architect Alex Possenbacher uses rich burnt umber-tinged shades of sunflower and deep corn that bring pueblo style to life. These colours are perfectly at home in the sun-filled setting of the Pacific Coast, where their roasting tones animate the coolest, darkest part of a house. With their warming burnt sienna content, they also work in spaces where there is a cooler, greyer light. Good for cooking and dining spaces, sunflower shades work well in outdoor rooms, verandahs or patios, where they bring instant sunshine to seating and food preparation areas.

THIS PAGE Rich golden tones applied as broken colour in a living room chime perfectly with a gilded fireplace, deep olive green woodwork and subtle tones – earthy brown on the furniture and deep reds on the carpet.

OPPOSITE Mexican architect Manolo Mestre has layered deep sunflower shades onto rough plaster in this light-filled home in Careyes on the Pacific Coast. Raw tones of burnt sienna and squab cushions in fuchsia bring further surprise and delight to this scheme.

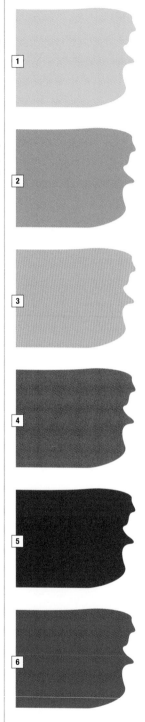

sunshine spectrum US designer

Jamie Drake's innate sense of colour simply sings in this warming bedroom
with its perfect saturated yellow walls and toning curtains. A yellow bed
throw and upholstered chairs tie the scheme together, while an eclectic mix
of wooden furniture creates a pleasing earth base for this rich palette.

chic adobe
Mexican architect Alex Possenbacher often uses indigenous colours such as rich yellow ochre on textured plaster surfaces to create layers of warm broken colour. Used on three-quarter walls in this vaulted bedroom, the strong tones are inviting rather than over-indulgent as they command attention without dominating the space.

1 Marigold
2 Brown Sugar
3 Pumice
4 New White
5 Texas Rose
6 Mississippi Mud

cranberry & orange

venetian rose
baby pink
strawberry milkshake
cherry blossom
rose garden
pink lipstick
candy floss
raspberry mousse
flame
coral
shrimp
tuscan red
nectarine
tangerine dream
carrot stick
russet
nasturtium
venetian red
mulberry
poppy
cherry
plaster pink
jaipur
pomegranate
sun-dried tomato
crimson
racing red
redcurrant
rich burgundy
chilli pepper
cadmium
moroccan red
ladybird
brick pink

ALL ABOUT RED

Red is powerful and evocative, sensual and symbolic, a primary colour that is confident and always ready to take a stand. Hot, fiery and passionate, it is an established favourite with designers, proving its versatility for adding space-enhancing comfort, conveying a bold design vision and providing life-affirming jolts of colour as accents.

In colour preference tests red is always more popular than yellow, green or orange. It has negative connotations too, though. Think about fire, flame and danger, or the colour of anarchy and revolution. On the one hand beware of its power and on the other, seize the moment and be brave with some purposeful shades. Red is the colour that women often cite as their favourite colour, whereas men are more likely to choose blue.

Red is an historical primary colour. Red paint, formed originally from naturally occurring red-oxide, was as popular in Pompeii as it was in Native American buildings. American barn red is a deep earthy red that endures today, as do the rich russet tones found in Swedish interiors on painted furniture and on vernacular buildings, often teamed with white woodwork.

You cannot help but react to rooms decorated with vibrant red. People who choose to decorate with this colour are often strong characters, with a zest for life and a need for excitement. Bold red shades will bathe a room with constant warmth, even one that does not receive much natural light, as well as increase adrenaline levels and raise blood pressure slightly on a first encounter.

Rich reds, the colours of red wine and roses, hearts and flowers, also promote energy, instil a sense of protection and offer a feeling of reassurance. All the assets of the red carpet

From raspberry to rose and tomato to tangerine, the red palette is fiery and fierce, courageous and passionate.

rolled into one if you like. And as a night-time colour, red is second to none, producing an enveloping reflective warmth. Many neutral colours are natural partners for reds, from pale biscuit and wheat to greys of varying intensity, from silver to slate. Even black brings out the vibrancy of red. It is a classic combination in Japanese interiors.

The drama queen of the colour palette, red is always dressed to impress.

From the softer shades of rose and baby pink, via coral and flame to the big bold ruby reds, the red palette works in small spaces as a saturated shade on all surfaces just as well as it does on one wall only, or as an accent colour in a larger space. It really comes into its own in analogous palettes though, where shades of red, rose and flame fall together in a loud statement or a subtle conglomeration, depending on the final mix of shades. Think of Campari and soda, the embers of a real fire, the ruby red shades of tomatoes or pomegranates. The reds of nature – colours of a sunset, soft fruits and poison berries, bright poppies and spotted ladybirds – are all able to mingle successfully in a room just as much as they do in nature.

In decoration, red traditionally often signified luxury, particularly when partnered with gilt or gold textures such as fringing or opulent picture frames. As red pigment was expensive until synthetic substitutes were discovered in the mid-19th century, its presence in state rooms, picture galleries and grand dining rooms was intended as a statement of wealth and exclusivity.

Calming the natural electricity of red is best done with pale neutrals. Clean white lends an instant Swedish feel, while buttery creams lend rustic charm and textured jutes and linens give a fresh contemporary country edge. If you want to increase the colour temperature even more though, add in a fresh zingy lime, in the form of temporary accessories such as a vase of *Alchemilla mollis* or a white dish of limes to create instant impact.

ROSE GARDEN

CANDY FLOSS

TUSCAN PINK

NECTARINE

MOROCCAN RED

MULBERRY

'When choosing colours, think about the colours you like to wear. Mixing colours is a form of expression and, if you like, a form of language; like the way one dresses.'

DAVID OLIVER, THE PAINT LIBRARY

USING RED Red is a versatile colour, looking crisp, contemporary and smart one minute when combined with textured slate grey upholstery, or simple and rustic when used in tomato shades as a strong accent colour on woodwork and furniture in an off-white room.

Red is a good analogous palette, working in partnership with crimson as it becomes deep plum or purple or before it merges into the green-blue and grey-blue. At the paler end of the spectrum, rosy tones ranging from muddy 1950s muted shades to more vibrant candy floss and rouge pink are perfect for feminine bedrooms and summery living rooms or kitchens, where sugar plum shades work well in combination with mint or leaf green, pale woods, deeper truer reds or a lilac palette. Introduce reds into a room in the form of luscious velvet curtains or vibrant cushions if you do not feel bold enough to make such a positive and dramatic colour statement by drenching your walls in saturated red tones.

David Oliver of the Paint Library feels strongly that one of the most common mistakes made when using deeper shades or strong colour on the walls is to paint the skirting board, cornice and architrave in too pale a shade. The effect to avoid is the sense of 'picture framing' or accentuating the perimeters or boundaries of a room with white woodwork. White surfaces are more visible to the naked eye than dark surfaces, which absorb light. As a guide try to keep the skirting board a shade not more than 50 per cent darker or lighter than the wall and floor colours so that the contrast is not too emphatic.

Red looks wonderful when partnered with any of the neutral colours, such as pale oaten beiges and greys to chocolate browns and deepest slate black.

Painting your woodwork in shades of red, when paired with walls in a compatible depth of colour, is a definite design statement.

Dining areas are often a good room in which to indulge a passion for deep red. The colour is known to make blood pressure rise slightly and the rush of adrenaline brings with it a heightened enjoyment of food and convivial conversation. North-facing rooms are positively warmed by red tones, especially in winter months.

Hotel designer Kit Kemp tends to use strong colours such as deep mulberry on walls that don't receive any light, such as basements and dark corners. 'I actually use contrasting strong colours on different walls to jolt the eye – we have done this with The Soho Hotel. This makes people forget that there is no actual daylight and also pulls your eyes round the corners. I also put a strong colour at the end of a corridor to pull your eye to what could be a very boring space.'

Bedrooms may not be the most ambient spaces for deep reds, as rest and relaxation may be hard to come by in such a stimulating environment. But dining rooms, living rooms and kitchens – which enjoy more activity – are all rooms that red likes. And hallways bathed in red will say a lot about you.

OPPOSITE TOP LEFT Layers of broken colour in shades of plaster pink and pale orange evoke the rough-textured walls of Tuscan farmhouses in Rupert Spira's London home.

OPPOSITE TOP RIGHT Shocking pink furniture accents provoke a strong harmony with vivid flame ceiling detailing in a contemporary apartment designed by Karim Rashid.

OPPOSITE BOTTOM Red and orange combine with one another surprisingly well, especially as accent colours in this cool, neutral space in Mexico, designed by Jenny Armit, which enjoys plenty of natural light.

With all the assets and symbols of the red carpet rolled into one, vigorous and assertive red calls for courage – wherever it is used, it makes its presence felt, so be prepared for it to dominate a room.

cranberry & orange | rose

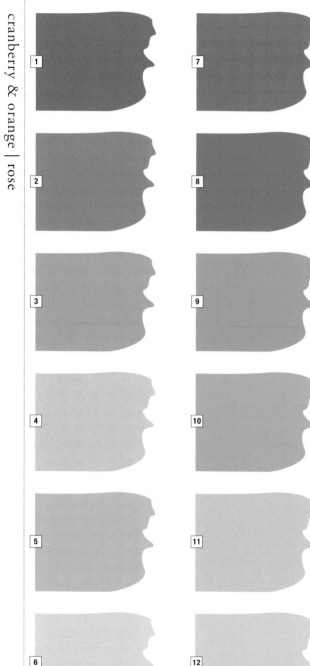

Feminine but not sugary rose pinks, hot flames in the form of rich oranges and, at the racy end of the spectrum, luscious reds make their presence felt.

ABOVE Dusky rose is a cool tone that absorbs light. It works well in rooms with plenty of natural light and in spaces where a colour lift is required.

1 Jaipur

2 Venetian Rose

3 Pink Lipstick

4 Pink Dream

5 Candy Floss

6 Sugar Almond

7 Tuscan Red

8 Rose Garden

9 Plaster Pink

10 Brick Pink

11 Strawberry Milkshake

12 Baby Pink

cranberry & orange | flame

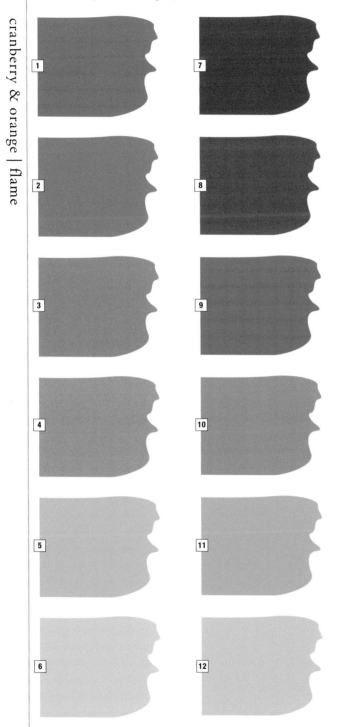

1 Tangerine Dream	**7** Cadmium
2 Paprika	**8** Crimson
3 Carrot Stick	**9** Moroccan Red
4 Nectarine	**10** Coral
5 Ochre Sand	**11** Freckle Flesh
6 Peach	**12** Faded Rose

cranberry & orange | redcurrant

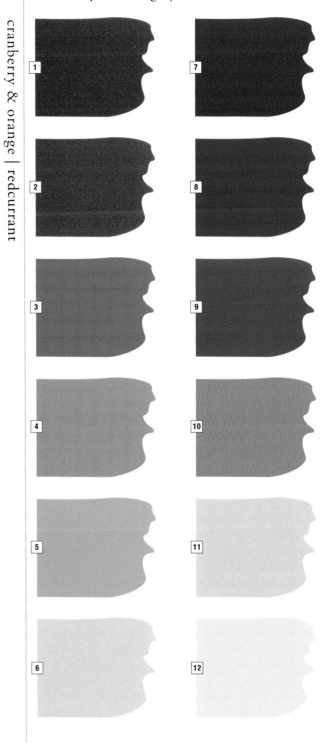

1 Racing Red	**7** French Claret
2 Chilli Pepper	**8** Rich Burgundy
3 Poppy	**9** Mulberry
4 Raspberry Mousse	**10** Pomegranate
5 Tuscan Pink	**11** Sherbet Pink
6 Silky Pink	**12** Antique Rose

'Farrow & Ball "Cinder Rose No. 246" is an unusual, fresh mauve-pink colour, which works wonderfully as a background to pictures and strong textiles – it is reminiscent of country house bedroom interiors. It has the attractive feeling of over-blown roses in an English garden in late summer: a really charming boudoir colour, sumptuous and opulent when contrasted with deep purples.' SARAH COLE, DIRECTOR, FARROW & BALL

rose

As delicate as a tea rose or as strong as a fuchsia in flower, rose tones are popular, not only for feminine bedrooms but also for breezy kitchens and airy living spaces. The red content in even the palest of baby pinks always provides a warm cast and an inviting ambience. Dusky muted tones work well in spaces that are used for contemplation, such as studies, libraries or quiet reading corners in a living room. Partner them with woodwork painted in sophisticated clotted cream shades or create a layered palette by using lavender blues or dusky grey mink in an analogous formation. Astonishingly popular as a colour for girls' bedrooms in recent years, rose has escaped the nursery and is now just as likely to be seen making a statement in kitchens, dining rooms and indeed bathrooms. Rose is also capable of being quite smart and sleek when accompanied by complementary shades of rich lime, forest green or mint, which are good colours for bringing out the best in the rose spectrum.

But if what you are aiming for is a delicate backdrop, then use analogous tones of soft peach and translucent coral and pair them with a pale steely grey or light tones of barely there mint for a sophisticated contrast. The paints of Farrow & Ball, Fired Earth and the Paint Library include perfect painterly pale pinks. Rose is a colour that is most successful when used in matt chalky form rather than as a glossy surface, which can make it appear too sickly, detracting from its natural grace.

THIS PAGE Faded tea-rose pink on walls, woodwork and furniture creates a delicate space in which a light teal green eiderdown evokes a 1930s colour palette. Feminine and inviting, this rustic bedroom is perfectly pink.

OPPOSITE Sugar plum paint on the walls creates a striking 'pink punch' background for fuchsia-toned fabrics and harmonious orange bedding. Reds, pinks and oranges always work surprising well together.

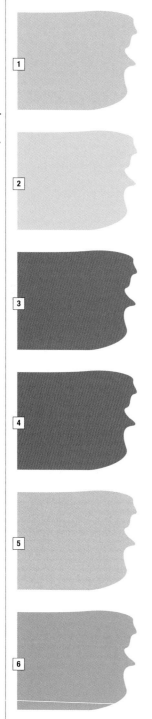

1 Strawberry Milkshake
2 Antique Rose
3 Military Uniform
4 Purple Heart
5 Lilac Grey
6 Gustavian

two-tone rose This exquisite period home

in the Canary Islands draws the clear light of the Atlantic Ocean into and
around its high-ceilinged rooms. A glorious mix of tone-on-tone roses,
faded lilacs and red-toned bleached boards makes for a wistful, pleasing
palette that changes through the day as the light travels around the space.

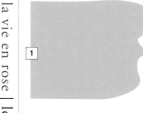

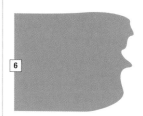

la vie en rose The Parisian home of designer

Agnès Comar employs the garden colours of traditional rose and green leaf
to punctuate a muted grey space. Slate grey sheers both frame the room and
allow diffused light to settle on the jewel-like chairs. The palette takes a
red/green complementary story to a pleasing, sophisticated level.

1 Venetian Rose
2 Mimosa
3 Gustavian Grey
4 Evening Dove
5 Kiwi
6 Lavender Blue

'Use signal colours like orange and cranberry to accentuate architectural detail. The use of contrasting colours is especially effective when they are used to highlight features such as arches, entrances, soffits, nooks and trim. This is an opportunity to play not just with colour but with dimensionality – have fun!'

CARL MINCHEW, DIRECTOR OF COLOR TECHNOLOGY, BENJAMIN MOORE

flame

THIS PAGE In John Pardey's Berkshire home he has painted one wall of a narrow corridor a vivid orange in direct contrast to its complementary colour, sea blue. Glimpsing the blue wall in the distance with an orange, warming atmosphere as you approach distracts attention from the narrowness of the space.

OPPOSITE In a French chateau, copper saucepans in rich, reflective tones look as though they were chosen to be displayed for the sole purpose of blending beautifully with the warm apricot colourwashed walls. A melodious mellow palette, perfectly accompanied by a scrubbed refectory table.

Hot, fiery and uncompromising, the orange story encompasses the vivid shades of tangerine, veering at one end of the spectrum dangerously close to overpowering pillar box reds and at the other to softer Tuscan tones. As with pink, vibrant orange shades can veer towards the tacky and unpleasant, so use them with care. Choose tones that contain a strong amount of brown in them for more of an earthy feel. For a vivid approach, use flame tones with a strong yellow element. Such strong shades never fail to enliven a space but are not for those whose forays into colour amount to a few muted neutrals. The flame palette packs a punch and makes a statement: just

think of the number of corporate companies who use orange in their brand identities to grab your attention, or the way 'safety' orange is used on the jackets of construction or rescue workers. It is therefore best to avoid using strong orange in rooms or places where you wish to create an aura of calm and relaxation.

Rich orange often looks best in tiny spaces such as guest cloakrooms. For a statement, allow a deep tangerine to make a grand appearance on one wall of a contemporary space. Architects of minimalist homes often use orange as a decorative element to break up and embolden brutalist linear rooms. As a warming tone, the deeper shades of russet and amber make great companions for a living space. Think of sun-kissed Italian villas, Provençal farmhouses and southwestern haciendas.

flame heaven

Striking flame is best saved for small surfaces and accessories. Here upholstery, a rug and a painting that includes orange square motifs are the starting point for an entire palette. With such strong accents, the walls must stay neutral so the furniture can do the colour talking.

flame heaven | opposite

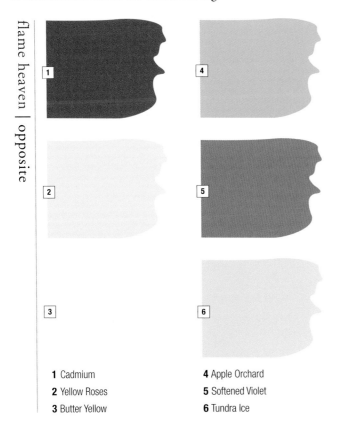

1 Cadmium	**4** Apple Orchard
2 Yellow Roses	**5** Softened Violet
3 Butter Yellow	**6** Tundra Ice

Fiery, passionate shades of orange are extremely good accent colours. Avoid bathing a whole room in these vibrant tones because they are most powerful when used in only part of a room.

tangerine dream

Burnt flame dado-height panels of colour anchor a scheme that comprises deep terracotta and cream chequerboard tiling and multi-coloured panes at the window. The result is warm, earthy and enriching, combining a pale but rich mascarpone shade on the walls and bedding with the rich rust.

tangerine dream | above

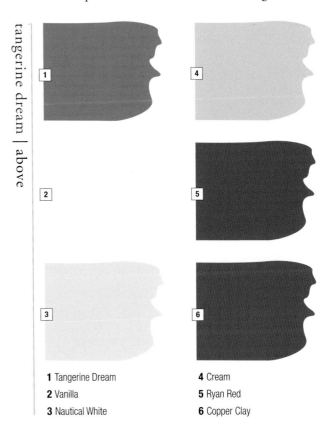

1 Tangerine Dream	**4** Cream
2 Vanilla	**5** Ryan Red
3 Nautical White	**6** Copper Clay

'Luscious and rich, hot reds bring an undeniable shot of life into any interior, whether the space is naturally dark or light. Powerful shades of deepest red, with their suggestion of fire and heat, bring an elemental quality to a room that cannot be ignored. These connotations of warmth make red the perfect shade for focal points around fireplaces and hearths.' ABRAHAM & THAKORE

THIS PAGE This Chinese-inspired palette in Charles de Sellier's house in Brussels includes deep claret walls set off by a heavy black marble fireplace and a collection of 1950s glass and ceramics. A pair of unusual low Chinese chairs in complementary wood complete the oriental scene.

OPPOSITE In a room that takes its style cue from Scandinavia, a bright cherry red wall brings life to an otherwise neutral room. Red and white punctuated with woody browns are always uplifting.

redcurrant

The devilishly rich shades of redcurrant comprise the fruity tones of cherry and tomato, through to a crop of crimson colours such as poppy and scarlet that are enriching and life-affirming. You cannot fail but feel welcome in a hallway or living room that is bathed in reflected red tones that are instantly warming, noisy and noticeable. Redcurrant is a great hit in northern climes, where its natural heat detracts from a lack of bright light. It will disguise a small space by making it feel enclosed but not claustrophobic, while in dining rooms rich reds stimulate conversation. The Chinese say that we should all have an accent of red in the house from which to gain

energy; they associate it with good luck and fortune. This can take the form of a vase of red roses or vibrant red berries, to a statement ruby red wall around a fireplace or framing a comfortable sofa. However you use it, the redcurrant palette is fun and enriching, an uplifting shade that reassures as it warms a space.

Redcurrant paired with the Night & Day shades of white, black or grey never fails to impress, giving a crisp but not cold combination of colours that sings with confidence and clarity. Before rushing to the paint pot, however, consider how much red you plan to use in a room. It is a colour that doesn't sit too happily with other shades not directly related to it and works best with subtle oranges, pinks or purples if used in a multi-layered colour story.

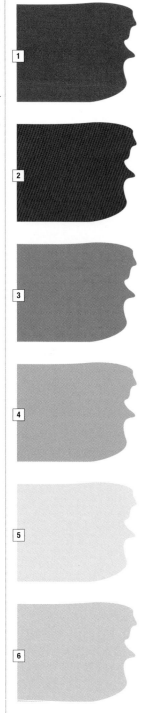

1 Racing Red
2 Charcoal
3 Paprika
4 Tuscan Pink
5 Salmon White
6 Strawberry Milkshake

feel the heat In a contemporary Indian home,

New Delhi fashion designers Abraham & Thakore employ audacious amounts of red. The red-pink sheers and a gloss finish on the floor and table allow the light to dance around the space and prevent the red from becoming overpowering. Slate grey and black act as counterpoints.

marrakesh express

Moroccan architect Karim el Achak uses enriching red on the smooth flat surface of a wall, where it absorbs light and creates mellow tones. Redcurrant tones well with shades of fuchsia, aubergine and sunny yellow.

hot coals

In another Karim el Achak interior the combination of rich red and deep slate grey is both sleek and reassuring. A stainless steel flue and berber rugs plus Moroccan artefacts in brass inject colour and texture into a contemporary living room.

marrakesh express | above

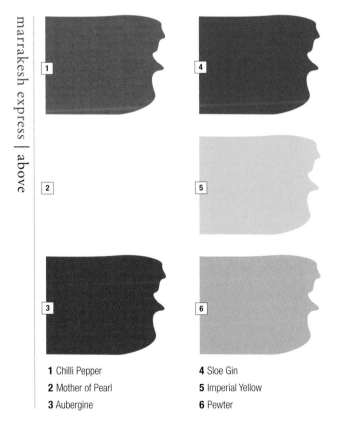

hot coals | above

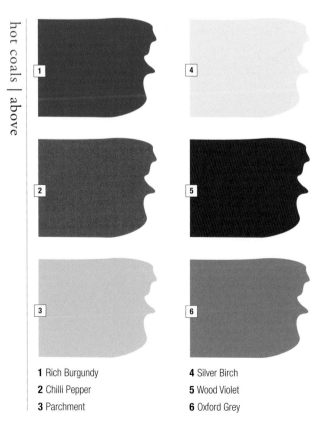

1 Chilli Pepper

2 Mother of Pearl

3 Aubergine

4 Sloe Gin

5 Imperial Yellow

6 Pewter

1 Rich Burgundy

2 Chilli Pepper

3 Parchment

4 Silver Birch

5 Wood Violet

6 Oxford Grey

lilac
& plum

grape
fig
blueberry
plum pie
radicchio
blackberry
boysenberry
deep purple
swiss chard
violet petal
sloe gin
bougainvillea
purple heart
crème de cassis
crocus
lavender blue
lilac
iris
french hydrangea
mauve sunset
vintage claret
rich ruby
magenta
marshmallow
misty rose
rioja
cyclamen
princess pink
passion flower
blush
sugar almond
pink peppermint
umbrian rose
electric pink

ALL ABOUT PURPLE

Purple is all about power and passion. Its strong and versatile hues are associated with creativity, individualism and inventiveness, perhaps by virtue of its changeable nature. Sitting between blue and red on the colour wheel, it speaks volumes and is not for the fainthearted or timid, as it is strident and symbolic. It ranges from amethyst and deep purple velvet tones to the faded fresco colours of light lilac or lavender. Purple can surprise and delight in equal measure. It is an enriching palette, whether it warms a space with tones so deep they are almost black in their intensity, or whether it projects light around a space via light-hearted lavenders and lacy lilacs that may be pale in tone, yet still add significant richness to a room by bathing it in a warm, subtle glow.

At the serious end of the spectrum, aubergine is chic, solemn and über-adult. It often works best as a rich accent, but a room bathed in purple is quite dramatic and surprisingly easy to live with, compared to some other strong colours. This deep velvety hue is a signature colour for French designers Michael Coorengel and Jean-Pierre Calvagrac, who love the way it reflects their combined passions for the baroque and the contemporary. They often use it on all four walls of a room and combine it with a quite startling analogous shade of rich coral.

The many shades of purple are uplifting yet calming; they are spiritual colours that promote innovation and warm a space. The Japanese associate purple with wealth and social standing, while in Egypt purple denotes virtue and faith. And of course purple is the main papal colour in the Vatican, closely related to both religion and serious ceremony. Purple has links with nobility. To be 'born to the purple' is to be born into a royal or noble family.

Purple is emboldened by red and blue, made delicate by an association with white or enveloped in passion by glossy finishes. It is a colour that is not afraid to talk out loud and takes strident steps by raising the colour temperature of a room.

The summery shades of pale lilac and lavender breathe light into dark spaces and a hint of sunshine into light ones. Although cheerful, these tones are astonishingly tricky to pin down. Always select a colour several shades lighter than the one you are aiming for, as they are more powerful when applied. Violet is the colour with the shortest wavelength on the spectrum, so it absorbs light easily. When viewed in sunny conditions it will appear more vivid and brighter in tone; artificial light will make it appear darker. Blue-tinged lilacs veer towards greyer colours, while red-tinged violets edge towards fuchsia.

Purple has always been a popular colour in the garden, where it has a calming effect and makes small gardens seem larger. Its natural affinity with whites, off-whites, linens and wheat tones outdoors translate well to the interior. Combining purples with these neutrals and introducing analogous tones of reds, whether vibrant or softer, pinker tones, together with blues in the form of denim or indigo creates really interesting palettes. Such combinations often linger in the visual memory thanks to their innate freshness and vitality.

Purple is more inviting than frightening. An emotive colour, it denotes power and justice, regal connections and a elegant front. Purples are passionate, romantic and seriously smart, and never go far out of fashion.

LILAC GREY

FIG

IRIS

'Lilac is one of my all-time favourite colours. I have incorporated its dreamy tones in my Denim fabric collection and even use it as a nail colour. Sanderson Paint's "French Lilac" is the most perfect shade for creating a warm and inviting bedroom or living room.'

LENA PROUDLOCK

BOYSENBERRY

MARSHMALLOW

SLOE GIN

USING PURPLE Purple is one of the most fascinating palettes to play with because it is so complex and versatile. It can be changeable in the paler tones, but in the solid, deeper tones it is a reassuring shade that anchors a space. Deep purples and pinks will definitely look better with a sheen, whereas a flat finish works well for the lighter shades.

Lavender reflects light really well so it is often used in rooms in northern Europe because it has a cheerful edge to it, even in the depths of winter. It can be deceptively strong, even in its paler shades, so experiment by applying it to a piece of lining paper and fix it to a wall where you want it to be. Watch it change throughout the course of a day before settling on a particular shade.

Geranium, slap bang in the middle of the spectrum, is really most at home where the sun is strong, just like the flower itself. Hot pinky purples are a sure-fire way of grabbing the eye, so use them as accents or if you don't mind having this saturated shade centre stage, then combine it with soft tones of cream or grey to divert attention elsewhere. Team it with acid green for a florid finish, but please only use the green in small quantities; otherwise, you will just succeed in jarring your senses.

Other shades that go well with purples include browns, greys and off-whites in all tints and tones. Reddish lilacs are quite geranium and pinky in tone, while bluish pale lilacs will head towards the grey end of the spectrum and become almost seascape in mood, giving a more ethereal feel and palette that is bluer overall.

Living rooms always look smart bathed in or accented by purple, as do dining rooms. Employ a full range of accent colours such as off-whites, wheats, greys, golds and browns for a smart finish. Purple's complementary partners range from shimmery gilt at the aubergine end of the spectrum through to acid green for geranium and lilac or yellow at the violet side of things. There is no denying that the analogous combination of purple and pink is a powerful and popular one, if a little too strong for my liking. Though gently done, in a way that apes the shades of pinky purple found in a garlic clove, this combination can produce a pleasing, not too punchy palette. While lilac and acid green can be quite slick if combined carefully, be watchful not to make too lurid a link by knocking back the brightness of the colours a little.

Kitchens, hallways and bedrooms all look good lined with lilac, especially when such rooms have a good supply of natural (but not necessarily bright or strong) light. Deep purples are best for dining rooms and living rooms, as well as bedrooms if you are feeling bold, as this colour will raise the emotional heat slightly. Children always appreciate rooms that are suffused with fun, bright colours, especially when they come from the geranium palette, while sunny garden rooms look great when decorated with lilac walls, white flowers and greenery or emboldened with one wall painted in a hot pink geranium colour. The more muted and reflective purple tones of grey-lavender, pale fig and peony sit well in any cosy, relaxing space.

Serene and interesting in living spaces, calm and contemplative in bedrooms, colours in the purple spectrum are equally at home in restful spaces as they are in dining and entertaining areas, appearing quiet or bold depending on the setting.

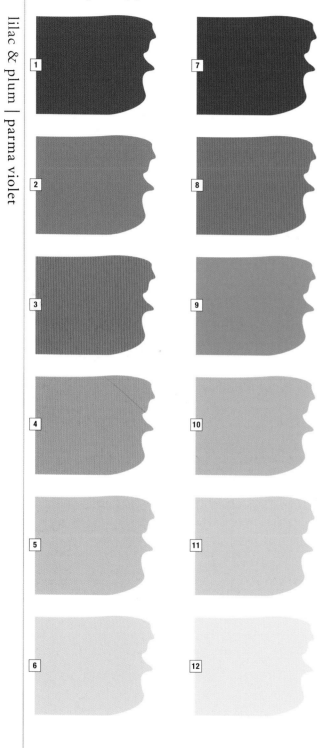

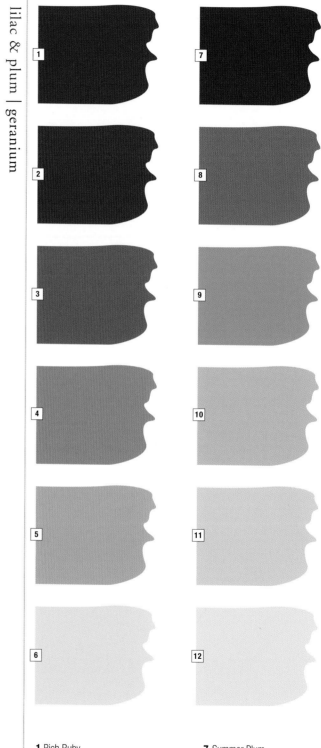

1 Deep Purple	**7** Modern Mauve
2 Iris	**8** Purple Heart
3 Crème de Cassis	**9** Lavender Blue
4 Mauve Sunset	**10** Crocus
5 French Hydrangea	**11** Lilac Grey
6 Spring Lilac	**12** Mauve Alabaster

1 Rich Ruby	**7** Summer Plum
2 Bougainvillea	**8** Passion flower
3 Sloe Gin	**9** Bright Lilac
4 Electric Pink	**10** Princess Pink
5 Umbrian Rose	**11** Marshmallow
6 Tea Rose	**12** Pink Peppermint

ABOVE French designers Michael Coorengel and Jean-Pierre Calvagrac take inspiration from both contemporary and baroque interiors. White cornice detailing and painted furniture allow the deep aubergine tones to come to the fore.

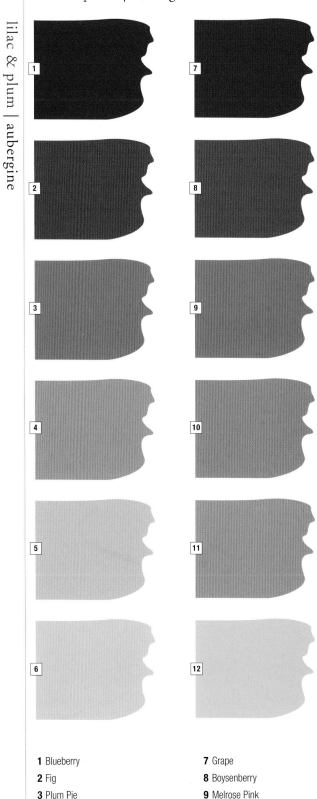

The colour purple ranges from the deep, strong aubergine shades at the powerful blue end of the story, through vivid geranium and hot pinky purples to the delicate shades of lilac and lavender where reds enter the palette.

1 Blueberry

2 Fig

3 Plum Pie

4 Faded Grape

5 French Grey

6 Violet Petal

7 Grape

8 Boysenberry

9 Melrose Pink

10 Cranberry Ice

11 Countryside Pink

12 Misty Rose

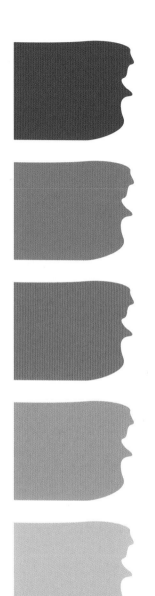

'Using purple with a pink edge adds feminine glamour and sophistication, which brightens up any room. These colours are enjoyable even on overcast days, and create a sense of nobility and independence. Dark purple is associated with royalty, dignity and transformation. Mixing in pink tones adds a hint of healing, femininity and sweetness.' JOHNNY GREY

parma violet

Lilac is best suffused with light so that its changeable nature can be fully appreciated. Versatile and interesting, the palest lilac that looks like only one or two shades on from a pale grey can look barely there one minute. Then, with the addition of generous natural sunlight or bright daylight, it will transmute into glorious lavender tones that are at once feminine and flattering. This is why when you are choosing a lilac colour it is really important to go several shades lighter than your intended colour, otherwise you will end up with a vile shade of tasteless mauve that will send shudders through your room. To prove the point, take a tear sheet of a room whose lilac colour you like and match it to a paint chart. It is always surprising with lilac just how terribly pale you have to go to get the right result. Lilac, when it is used in exactly the right way, is light-enhancing and delicate rather than bright and brash.

For inspiration, consider the appealing shades of old-fashioned parma violets, the pinky blue of the hydrangea head and the richer tones of a Provençal lavender field. Vital and uplifting, these soft shades are perfectly pinkish but not twee.

Use lilacs in kitchens and hallways to appreciate how much their colours vary throughout the day. They work well in bedrooms, too, bringing a fresh and sunny atmosphere with them, even in northern light. Essentially spring and summer colours, lilacs are nevertheless perfectly pleasing year round.

THIS PAGE Hilton McConnico's Paris apartment is a symphony in lilac without being overpowering. Fresh, clean tones of parma violet on walls, curtains and even candelabras are punchy and inviting. A dark wooden floor provides a good counterpoint.

OPPOSITE This tranquil and inviting bedroom was decorated to complement a series of colour field paintings in the home of Nicholas Alvis Vega and Liza Bruce. Three harmonious tones of parma violet, pale mauve and deep lilac, applied in horizontal bands from dark to light up the wall, demonstrate just how much natural light these colours absorb. The paler tones almost merge into the darker shades where the light is brightest.

multi-layered
In a house designed by Don Chapell, kitchen units are painted in a subtle colour palette of sea greens, soft pink earth and pale lilacs. Each of the shades relates to the tones and hues found in the surrounding landscape in Sarasota, Florida.

kitchen zing
Sharp citrus lime chimes well against a wall of lavender and kitchen cabinets in pale-toned beech wood in a classic case of how the right accent colour can bring both definition and visual interest to a palette.

multi-layered | above

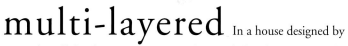

1

4

2

5

3

6

1 Lilac Grey

2 Mauve Sunset

3 Mauve Finesse

4 Lime Twist

5 Celadon

6 Spring Lilac

kitchen zing | above

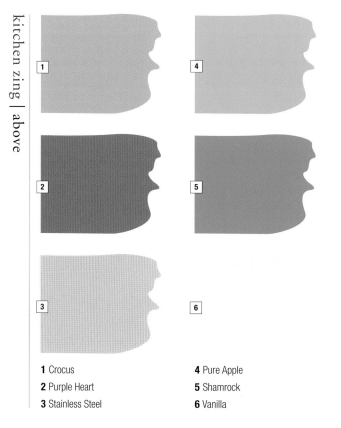

1

4

2

5

3

6

1 Crocus

2 Purple Heart

3 Stainless Steel

4 Pure Apple

5 Shamrock

6 Vanilla

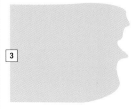

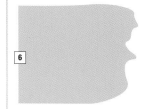

cool dining At the opposite end of the

kitchen shown top left on the opposite page, a dining area is painted in the same colour but in differing proportions to provide a lively eating space. Beech dining chairs and shades ranging from deep purple to pale lavender combine to make the mood sharp, fresh and fun.

1 Lavender Blue
2 Cornflower Blue
3 Mint Tea
4 Barley
5 Fig
6 Sunset

'Floral, exciting, powerful, alive, positive and really uplifting – use strong geranium shades with electric oranges or lime green for a perfectly complementary story or calm the space with pure whites and silver highlights. Always optimistic and pleasurable, geranium is a rich colour that enhances white spaces and adds soft warmth to small rooms.' KARIM RASHID

geranium

Geranium embraces the reddish tones of purple and the hot pinky tones of red to create a vivid rosy spectrum that includes fuchsia and bougainvillea. In hot countries it works beautifully on walls; in cooler climates, use it with care and vary the shades so one colour doesn't dominate a space. Fuchsia accents look strong but not overpowering in neutral spaces, on paintings and cushions.

American designer Jamie Drake often employs hot pinks on walls and accessories – indeed it is one of his favourite colours. Such strong tones can work successfully when limited to one wall of a room. Combine them with dusky grey-pinks to add a layer of subtlety and prevent the pink from grabbing all the attention. And use further analogous shades of amethyst and intense purples to provide drama and gravitas.

Combine geranium with steely greys as a foil for the brightness, or keep the story fresh by adding in rose-tinged whites and pearly off-whites. For sheer fun, you can use geranium shades on walls in the garden, where they will be absorbed by the sun and provide a suitably lush backdrop for a panoply of rich greenery.

In bathrooms geranium is a particularly successful colour, as its pink/red tones will enhance your skin tone and therefore improve how you feel when you look in the mirror each morning. Rich shades on the walls here are capable of setting your mood for the day, so don't be afraid to embrace the feminine in the bathroom.

1 Rich Ruby
2 Electric Pink
3 Pine Sprigs
4 Pink Peppermint
5 Blue Orchid
6 Mighty Aphrodite

casa viva
A serene, all-white bed is canopied in a deep pink sheer curtain and backed by a deep raspberry crush wall that provides strong definition in the room as well as anchoring the bed. Pink-tinged grey stone flooring and a sherbet-coloured contemporary day bed nod to the red end of the spectrum while still providing contrast.

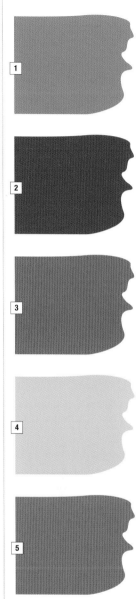

rich in pink
A Manhattan apartment bathed in designer Jamie Drake's signature strong colours is unmistakeably glamorous and appealing. The colour cue for the dining room scheme comes from the painting, all of whose colours are represented somewhere in the room, whether in the decoration or the furniture and accessories.

1 Electric Pink
2 Rich Ruby
3 Bright Lilac
4 Cheetah
5 Blueberry
6 Silver Mink

'Farrow & Ball "Pelt No. 254" is a rich plum-brown, lighter and less red than Farrow & Ball's "Brinjal", but with the same dramatic effect; it has something of the natural tones of dark animal fur. Pelt is incredibly versatile and will change dramatically in effect and impact when contrasted with other colours and when used in varying lights.' SARAH COLE, DIRECTOR, FARROW & BALL

aubergine

THIS PAGE Deep aubergine walls make a handsome colour story together with faded olive and oak steel-framed vintage canteen dining chairs.

Dark purple can make a room appear larger than life, making the walls and ceiling disappear, so is a good colour to use in small spaces. It is also good for creating intimacy, so is equally at home in cosy living spaces as it is in romantic bedrooms. If the thought of rooms bathed in purple seems too much, then consider using it sparingly, by applying it below dado height or on one wall only, then add in smaller elements such as vases or cushions, throws and lampshades. Deep purples lend themselves to glossy and reflective surfaces, so use them on velvets and silk drapes and upholstery as well as on softly glossy walls. This is the one colour that does not work quite so well when applied in matt, murky shades.

Purple blues such as rich midnight and deepest cobalt are seriously sexy colours that are just right in dining rooms that call for smart evening entertaining. Introduce some glossy gilt tones in the form of mirrors or shimmering glassware and add in some soft lighting and you will succeed in creating a touch of Hollywood glamour and a perfect mood.

Living rooms always look smart bathed in or accented by purple, while kitchens, hallways and bedrooms prefer lilac or geranium shades. Children's rooms, which always enjoy bright colours, will benefit from purple, and sunny garden rooms look great suffused with lilac walls, white flowers and greenery.

OPPOSITE Dado-height panels of deep plum topped with a thin stripe of royal red provide a rich and subtle anchor for an otherwise minimally furnished bedroom.

regal elegance

Deep purple combined with vivid cranberry red and turquoise green accents, plus white counterpoints on picture frames and freestanding sculpture, demonstrate how a successful palette can work using clashing colours.

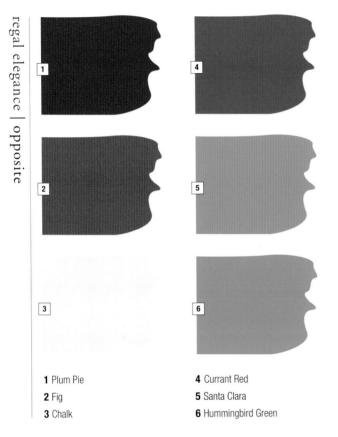

1 Plum Pie

2 Fig

3 Chalk

4 Currant Red

5 Santa Clara

6 Hummingbird Green

Deep purple enriches a space, providing a backdrop for shades of gilt, olive and vivid reds. It is a colour that works in small spaces and larger rooms, in contemporary and traditional settings.

reading room

This kitchen and living area has storage space disguised behind deep plum, push-catch sectioned cupboards that provide an interesting glossy colour panel while doubling up as a space divider within the room.

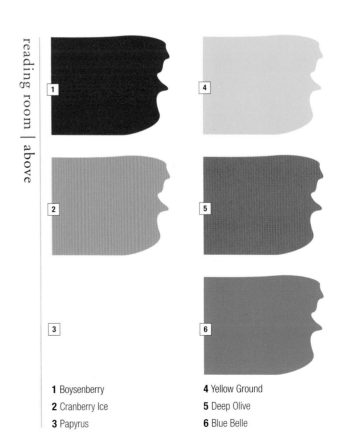

1 Boysenberry

2 Cranberry Ice

3 Papyrus

4 Yellow Ground

5 Deep Olive

6 Blue Belle

sea
& sky

hibiscus
rockpool
azure
seaspray
cornflower
shoreline
mexico
duck egg
indigo
caribbean
midnight blue
wedgwood
beach shack
steely sky
kingfisher
mediterranean
denim
sapphire
ultramarine
prussian blue
turquoise
lapis
delft
bayberry
riviera
powder blue
gustavian
aquamarine
shaker blue
periwinkle
hawaiian sea
cobalt
forget-me-not
hyacinth

ALL ABOUT BLUE

Blue denotes comfort, security and peacefulness. It is everywhere in nature and therefore suits us well. The blue palette evokes the sea and the sky, with calm elemental colours that lend watery tones and nautical connotations to an interior. Blue is versatile, whether with the cooler hues of sky and duck egg or the interesting, mysterious blue-greys that may verge on the slightly austere, but are nevertheless soulful and graceful.

Basing palettes on the naturally occurring colours of the coastal path always produces a pleasing result, as whenever you reproduce one of nature's palettes, the colours always work. They feel at home with one another. Think of wheat grass swaying wistfully against a stormy sky, melancholic seaspray lapping against clam shells on a pebble beach, or mottled ochre sand against a pale autumn sky. These are the ethereal sea and sky colours that are contemplative yet easy on the eye, creating an instant sense of calm and wellbeing.

At the brighter end of the spectrum vivid tones of cobalt and turquoise are joyous colours, most at home in southern climes, where the strong sunlight brings out their rich hues and keeps them looking bright but not garish. They need the sun to bring out their deep colour; in the northern hemisphere they can look very cold. Use the stronger shades of denim, periwinkle and jewel-bright turquoise or aquamarine as accents for maximum impact without overkill. These are powerful, enriching shades when used with restraint.

Florida, California and Mexico are the perfect settings for strong blues, but further north they only really work as accent colours, turquoise especially. In Europe, and particularly in the UK, it is best to 'dirty up' blue tones to soften them and give them warmth. Duck egg and pale Provençal blue look wonderful here when they have just enough grey and burnt umber in them to dull their sheen. Elusive and delicate, the elegant tones of duck egg and teal work in the same way as a filigree fretwork screen provides elegant tracery in a space – they allow light to subtly bounce around and create a soft, clear sheen around a room. Think of 18th-century Gustavian interiors from Sweden.

The classic crisp navy and white nautical palette, so often used in bathrooms, shower rooms and seaside living spaces, always looks fresh and appealing, although it is best to choose some creamy, dreamy off-whites to accompany true navy. They are still crisp-looking but somehow more inviting than pure white. Mix in some linen colours too, such as shades of grey fisherman's rope or jute, to soften the atmosphere.

Sky tones include elegant Wedgwood blue, which works well punctuated with a shot of red for a fresh, lively bedroom. Or tone it down with a knocked-back white, like the china itself, for an elegant but not chilly result.

From the classic combination of china blue and ice white to delicate shades of egg shell and seaspray, blue is uplifting and refreshing, harmonious and welcoming.

Blue's complementary colour, yellow, works best when tweaked along the colour spectrum away from too vivid a sunflower yellow if it is to be combined with a strong shade of blue. From pale sand at one end to an enriching ochre at the other, this is a good range in which to form a palette. The overused combination of bright blue and bright yellow, while an enduring classic and a combination that was frequently used in kitchens some 20 years ago, looks a little tired these days. It's far more exciting to experiment at the paler end of the spectrum. Blue and white has often been a colour theme for kitchens, thanks to the blue and white china traditions extending from Chinese to Wedgwood and Cornishware.

MEXICO

AQUAMARINE

POOLSIDE

'From palest aqua blue to Caribbean cabina indigo, the colours of the sea and the sky are infinitely varied and evocative. Use paler shades with caramel and sand or make complementary statements with blue and shades of red. For harmony, layer a room with tones of blue-grey, cornflower and soft neutrals.' ANN GRAFTON, MANAGING DIRECTOR OF GP & J BAKER

COBALT

GUNMETAL BLUE

MILITARY UNIFORM

Blue never fails to enliven the spirit and lift the soul. Popular and peaceful, it is the perfect weekend colour, promoting calm and recuperation.

USING BLUE Blue is the signature colour for many a room. It is capable of being bright and breezy, moody and elusive or deep and mysterious, depending on the range of shades used. One of the most popular colours around, it invariably refreshes and revives the senses.

Sea and sky colours range from the pale blue-greys of driftwood and leaden seascapes to crisp, clear summer skies and the turquoise glory of a Caribbean ocean to deep stormy midnight blues, almost as black as night.

The Shakers often used a shade of blue named Heavenly Blue that is a cross between a deep Provençal cornflower blue and navy. It was used to paint furniture and on woodwork and always looked crisp against the wheaten tones of handcrafted pine furniture. Heavenly indeed.

Shipshape and nautical, classical blue and white schemes in which the paler colours provide accents veer from the Cornishware blue and cream to the ever popular navy and white stripes of Breton vests and the sharp maritime navy that tones so well with true white. While a strictly nautical scheme can be somewhat predictable and perhaps a little cold, it is interesting to steer

Use the nautical palette as a starting point but shift the colour boundaries to create new partners – turquoise and imperial yellow, sky blue and coral, powder blue and biscotti.

the combination in different directions for slightly more adventurous results. Ralph Lauren has made the nautical palette his own by taking a subtle approach to maritime associations and using pencil-thin navy lines on ticking fabrics against antique white walls. The result is a restrained coastal style that always looks fresh.

Sky blues, for instance, make good partners for steely grey whites, as well as their perfect partners of sand and corn shades that lend a fresh, summery and coastal edge. Blue taken to a semi-turquoise level will appear elegant against ice-white architectural detailing or upholstery. Accent this with a striking imperial yellow and you will see a jewel-like contrast that will pop with life. Silver and gold work wonders against pale blues, bringing a sharp edge and reflective planes that enrich the clear tones of the blue.

Denim blues or those that look best in matt, chalky tones such as moody grey-blues work well in bathrooms, especially so when combined with dusky pinks that have a strong element of red in them. Or use coral for a slightly softer accent.

The rich and more vibrant ocean shades of azure, periwinkle or aqua require more sensitive handling. Team them with dark wood shades rather than pure white to best effect. Watery, rockpool blues always work with iridescent surfaces, so think about introducing shimmery silk fabrics, china or glass that plays with the light or some sleek, glossy silvery blues in the form of blue-on-blue tones. Experiment with two tones of wall colour, blue accents in the form of cushions and let the colours create a harmonious collection of shades that meld into one another.

OPPOSITE TOP LEFT
Perfect sky blue walls are both fresh and restful. Here they make a calming palette combined with furniture and a bedhead in sandy shades designed by Bill Mostow.

OPPOSITE TOP RIGHT
Seascape colours include moody sky tones as well as uplifting brights. In Agnès Emery's Moroccan house, slate-blue painted furniture has a subtle quality, changing tones as sunlight moves around the house throughout the day.

OPPOSITE BOTTOM LEFT
Designers Carlos Mota and Miles Redd have employed a succulent royal blue to create a cosy intimacy in this period living room in New York.

OPPOSITE BOTTOM RIGHT Undersea tones collide in a watery-inspired mix of Caribbean blue and sunny aqua in this bedroom scheme.

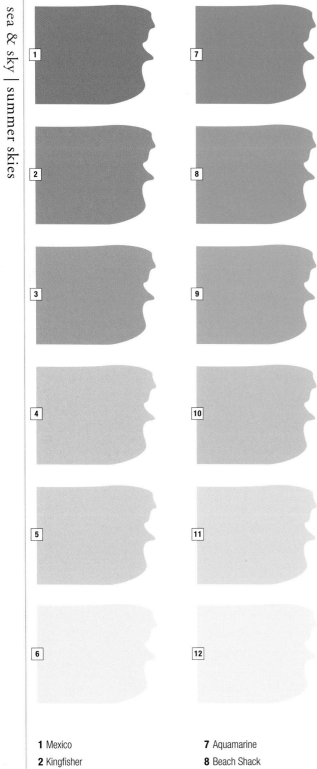

1 Mexico

2 Kingfisher

3 Forget-me-not

4 Rockpool

5 Wedgwood

6 Delft

7 Aquamarine

8 Beach Shack

9 Turquoise

10 Shoreline

11 Grey Day

12 Duck Egg

Sea and sky colours are some of the most popular, uplifting and endlessly variable tones to decorate with. Strong, calming and trustworthy, they are dependable but not dull, dynamic but not overpowering.

ABOVE This pale neutral scheme is defined and completed with a painted French window in duck egg blue, and one wall painted in an ethereal sky blue to provide impact, warmth and depth in an otherwise understated space.

sea & sky | ocean

sea & sky | ocean

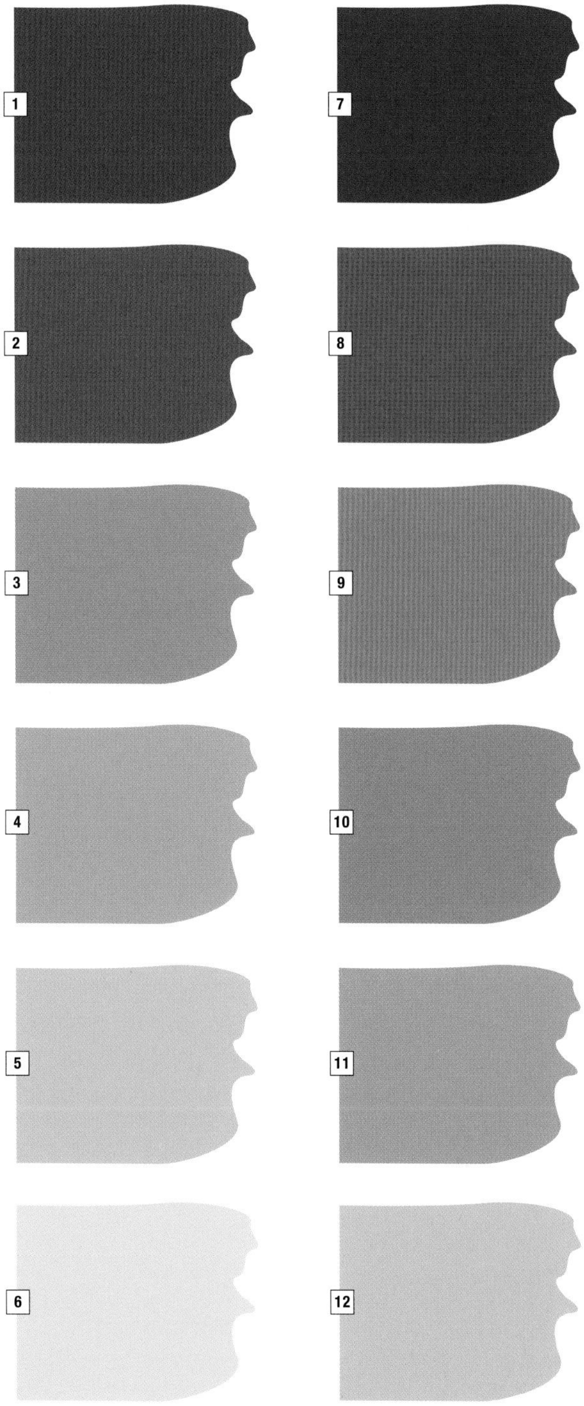

1 Prussian Blue
2 Cobalt
3 Periwinkle
4 Faded Denim
5 Cool Blue
6 Ice Blue
7 Midnight Sky
8 Shaker Blue
9 Poolside
10 Cabina
11 Athenian Blue
12 Hawaiian Breeze

sea & sky | stormy

sea & sky | stormy

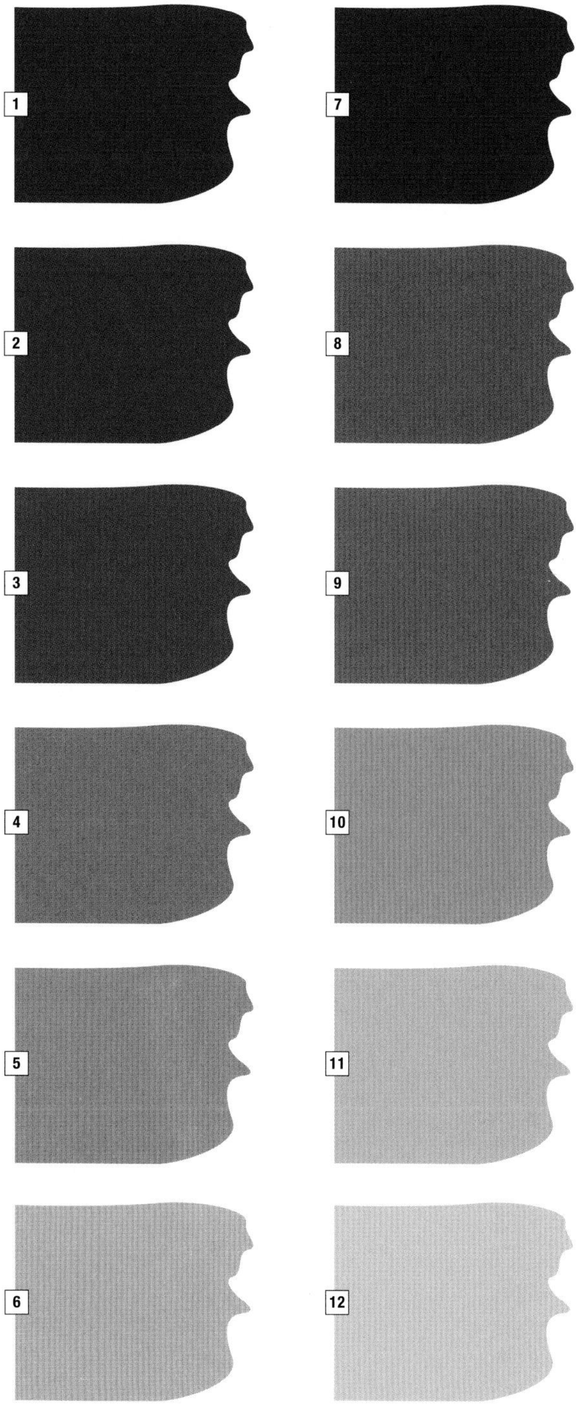

1 Midnight Blue
2 Moonlight
3 Deep Navy
4 Pebble Grey
5 Steely Sky
6 Wedgewood Grey
7 Evening Sky
8 Gunmetal Blue
9 Military Uniform
10 Harlequin Blue
11 Gustavian
12 Blue-Grey

'Ralph Lauren's "River Rapids WHO3B" is white with the palest tint of blue. I used it on the interior walls of my cabinets in the dining room. My collection of old silver shimmers off of it. It is very similar to the background colour of my blue and white Chinese export china. It is also the perfect colour for a ceiling in a brown or white room.' ALEX BATES, WEST ELM

THIS PAGE Crisp, clean cornflower blue set against pale primrose and a warm white delights the eyes and senses with a summery feel.

OPPOSITE Palest sky blue is heightened by shafts of natural light that bounce around the room and evoke sunny days by the coast.

summer skies

Summer sky blue is often mistaken as a cold colour, but as long as it has a certain amount of magenta or purple in its base it can be wonderfully soft, warming and uplifting, especially in bedrooms and living rooms.

Keeping blues warm is a matter of applying a shade with warm tones in it and teaming it with rich sandy shades that echo the seashore, or else crisp whites, cool greys and palest yellows. Pale clear blue also looks fabulous combined with oak or chestnut furniture, which serves to keep the atmosphere warm rather than cool.

White is the perfect foil for this colour as it apes the summer skyline, bringing freshness to a summery palette. Provide shots of additional colour by adding tomato red or acid green accents in the form of flowers, fabrics or china for extra zing. The classic combination of blue and white is a perennial favourite and is endlessly adaptable. Cornish blue and cream, Greek Island sky and ice white, pale topaz and buttermilk are all variations on a classic core palette that shift subtly yet produce transforming nuances in a palette. The key to success is to use soft off-whites with a touch of magenta or grey in them so the white is not too punchy, as this would bring out the coldness in the blue.

These colours and combinations are adaptable enough to suit any room, from bedrooms to kitchens. They work best in spaces that benefit from generous natural light, but can survive in both the north and the south.

rich wood
Earth tones of oak wood ground an ethereal pale blue in a smart living/dining area, while accents of reddish pink and sand warm up the space. Pale blue and wood, ranging from pale beech to deep mahogany is a winning combination.

manhattan cool
Busts on pedestals provide white contrast in this library/dining room in a New York apartment, where jewel-like accents of warm lime and bright turquoise, together with lilac alliums, are set against Wedgwood blue walls.

rich wood | above

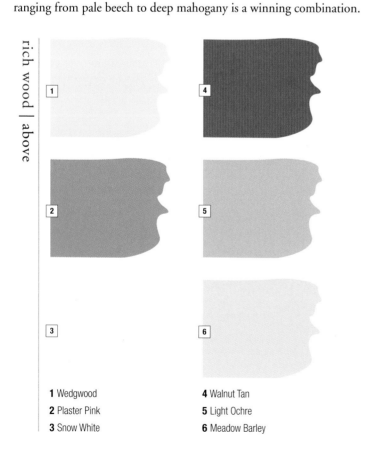

manhattan cool | above

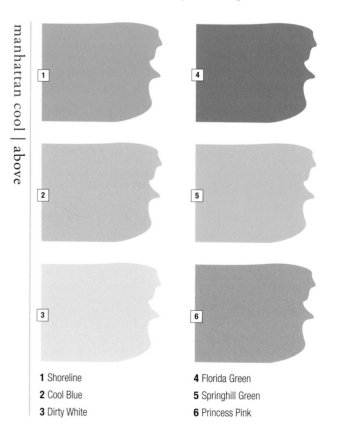

1 Wedgwood

2 Plaster Pink

3 Snow White

4 Walnut Tan

5 Light Ochre

6 Meadow Barley

1 Shoreline

2 Cool Blue

3 Dirty White

4 Florida Green

5 Springhill Green

6 Princess Pink

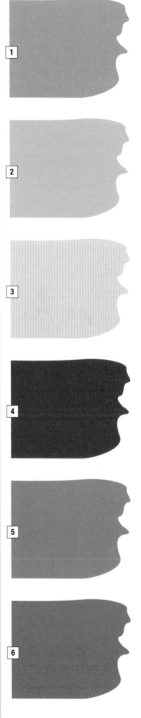

1

2

3

4

5

6

provençal dining Clear-toned
walls and white woodwork provide a fresh backdrop to this sunny area
for dining and entertaining. Red and pink counterpoints on the multi-
patterned fabric seat covers on the chairs and the accessories complete
this understated nautical scheme of blue, white and red.

1 Rockpool
2 Kingfisher
3 Blue-Gray
4 Ladybird Red
5 Genuine Pink
6 Moroccan Red

china corner

Everyone loves blue and white rooms. Charming baby blue walls are a perfect complementary statement for the creamware jugs and classic country blue-and-white tableware displayed on a painted dresser. Accent tones in wheaten grey, rich buttermilk and gunmetal grey also sit well together.

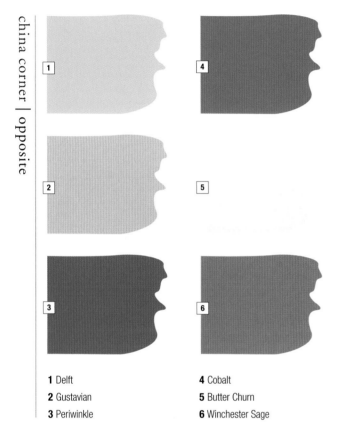

1 Delft

2 Gustavian

3 Periwinkle

4 Cobalt

5 Butter Churn

6 Winchester Sage

Invigorating and informal, this smart palette is just right for coastal settings and anywhere that needs a cheery uplift. Shades ranging from lilac-blue to rich Wedgwood blue-grey all work well.

coastal calm

Powder blue woodwork on the chair and closet doors, sky blue and deeper grey walls and a glossy floor of biscuit tones are defined and edged with plain white stripes and punctuated with redcurrant red and hints of hyacinth. This is truly a crisp and easy-living palette for sea lovers everywhere.

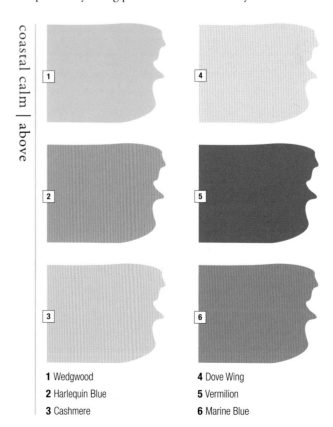

1 Wedgwood

2 Harlequin Blue

3 Cashmere

4 Dove Wing

5 Vermilion

6 Marine Blue

'The one element to consider when you choose your palette is the style and period of the building and, more importantly, its geographical context (urban or country, climate, natural light). For example, the summery blue I chose as a dominant colour for my house in Marrakesh was not chosen because we are near the sea. This is the exact shade that is offered in the streets of the medina.' AGNÈS EMERY, EMERY & CIE

ocean

The denim and azure colours of deep royal blue and deep watery greeny blues are persistently popular colours to decorate with. The Caribbean-inspired turquoise and azures are often the colours that are craved in wintery northern light, but they really do not work there. What looks fabulous on a Caribbean holiday does not readily translate to a London or New York home. Jewel-like aqua may sit happily in a Bahamas living space, but it in fact needs strong sun to appear so alive. In the north it would simply seem cold and out of place.

Vivid royal blues, inspired by the Mediterranean sea colours, look wonderful pared with matt, chalky, 'sad' greys, which provide a calming counterpoint. Or use them in a workspace, studio or home office against linen white woodwork for a punchy, uplifting space.

On the other hand, denim and electric blues are perfect for those places where the light is not bright. Because they look dirtied up, with elements of chalky grey or earth tones as part of their core colour, they absorb light and change with the quality of the light over the course of the day or when placed under artificial light. This mutability will make it seem as though the walls are 'talking' to you. These tones are perfect for making a strong colour statement in a dining area or even a kitchen, used as a wall colour against pale beech or ash cupboards. In fact, they work well with wood of all tones, from limed oak to rich cherrywood.

THIS PAGE Deep tones of rich ocean blue on the walls are sharply complemented with smart contemporary lighting and office furniture in this home office in Helsinki designed by Ulla Koskinen. White woodwork and ceiling, together with a pale beech floor, break up the colour and allow light to reflect off it.

OPPOSITE In Agnès Emery's home in Marrakesh the kitchen is in the open air, so tiles are a practical way of introducing colour. Vivid tiled walls in jewel-bright ocean tones provide a reflective surface for natural light, and merge well with matt grey-painted cupboards.

1 Prussian Blue
2 Winter Gates
3 Silver Birch
4 Secluded Beach
5 Noisette
6 Classic Brown

spanish modern This Ibizan retreat

designed by Ramón Esteve is bathed in natural light, painted
white with polished concrete floors, and furnished with iroko wood and
steel for the ultimate cool living in a hot climate. Jolts of ocean blue on
one wall in several rooms allude to the sea that surrounds the house.

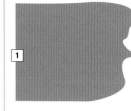

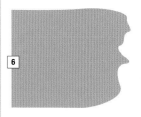

turquoise twist A moody autumnal

sea colour is well counterpointed with shades of wheatgrass, weather-beaten
sand and red rocks. Quiet and contemplative, this is a good palette for a
bedroom as it provides a calming atmosphere. Blues and browns are ever-
present on coast and creekland, in differing intensities.

1 Athenian Blue
2 Delft
3 Ochre
4 Great White
5 Greenfield Pumpkin
6 Roxbury Caramel

'To create a soothing atmosphere in the dining room I used warm materials in deep shades of aubergine, grey, black and taupe. This carefully chosen, rich palette was mixed to create an elegant room, with the bold shades adding elegance and interest. These shades are understated and subtle, which is why they recur in my interiors.' LUIGI ESPOSITO

THIS PAGE Midnight blue walls and painted cupboards provide a receding backdrop in a bedroom where white bed linen and an oak bedside table provide the visual focus. Designer John Minshaw has put together an unusual but successful colour palette for a bedroom.

OPPOSITE Designer Luigi Esposito has created a sense of glamour using stormy night-sky colours. The scheme is particularly successful after dark, when the textured walls absorb any natural light in the room and light from the chandeliers places the emphasis on the dining area.

stormy

Rich, exotic blues are undergoing a renaissance in home décor. These versatile deep shades make great bases and accents, and can be used in many tones and fabrics for everything from elegant to ethnic. Midnight blue is the decorators' favourite for night-time dining rooms. It is at its best with soft lighting, candles, gleaming silverware and white table linen. For less formal rooms, midnight blue can be used as a background colour to contrast with almost any hue – sugar plum pink and creamy whites; all the shades of pale to mid blues; and even sharp green.

The dark, stormy shades also team well with other blues and greens and earth tones, especially coffee shades. They can be used extensively in living areas and also make fine accent colours, particularly in the form of glass and china or sumptuous velvet drapes. As with all rich colours, experiment a little on a small area before you leap in, as it is important to assess the impact of such a dramatic colour. Stormy blues work well in northern light; they have been dirtied up so don't need natural light to enhance the warmth.

It is hard to underestimate the importance of small contrasting colours that complement the main palette of a room. For instance, vibrant yellow flowers look wonderful with blue, or choose small sunflower cushions against navy upholstered furniture for a jolt of interesting colour. Unexpected fabrics on a dark oak table will lend a new level of interest, as will carefully chosen rugs in neutral shades.

1 Gunmetal Blue

2 Gunmetal

3 Silver Birch

4 Plum Pie

5 Ansonia Peach

6 Titanium White

wedgwood blues John Minshaw has

taken the classic darker Wedgwood blue and created a sophisticated palette
by combining it with a porcelain white, then accenting it with golden tones
in the form of gilt mirrors and gilt-edged historical portraits. A soft mauve
used on the upholstery of oak-framed chairs echoes the golds elsewhere.

grey skies
This Moroccan bathroom, designed by Paris-based Agnès Emery, is a story based around stormy sunrise and sunset tones – fierce mauve-oranges, steely grey clouds and muddy blue tones. Ironically, moody colours produce a serene palette.

cool cuisine
In designer Axel Vervoordt's Belgium home the matt, stormy blues are confined to accents, used on ceiling beams, window frames and painted chairs, to give an overall impression of muted blue. The terracotta tiles provide warmth.

grey skies | above

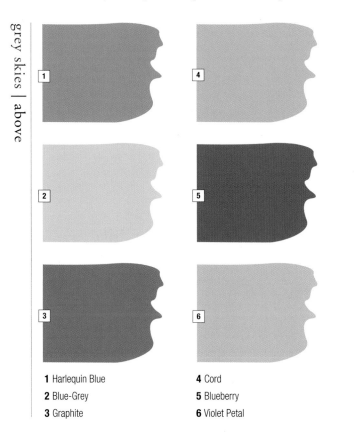

cool cuisine | above

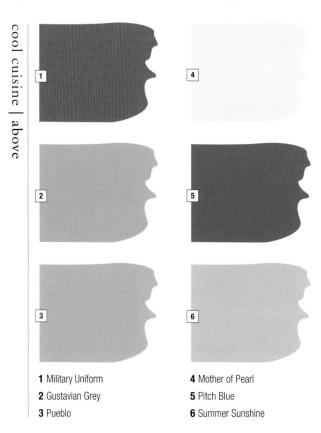

1 Harlequin Blue
2 Blue-Grey
3 Graphite
4 Cord
5 Blueberry
6 Violet Petal

1 Military Uniform
2 Gustavian Grey
3 Pueblo
4 Mother of Pearl
5 Pitch Blue
6 Summer Sunshine

avocado
& pistachio

emerald
jade
prickly pear
pine tree
endive
pine woods
cool mint
love bird
sage
coriander
celadon
chameleon
khaki
zuccini
amazon
pear
lime twist
meadow
concombre
gothic green
herb garden
olive tree
mint tea
dew
chrome green
cooking apple
brunswick green
mint chocolate chip
forest
chicory tip
spring greens
moss
bramley
fern

ALL ABOUT GREEN

Green is popular right now, and for all the right reasons. Its close association with all things natural and sustainable means that it has made a big interiors comeback of late. From the pleasing translucent tones of pale celery and delicate pistachio to the reassuring lime and forest tones at the richer end of the spectrum, green provides nurture as well as nature. A relaxing, enriching and comforting colour, it symbolizes growth, harmony and fertility.

As a secondary colour, formed by mixing blue and yellow, greens can be pushed to either ends of the spectrum. Yellowy greens can be temperamental and not always easy to work with, as they are capable of looking sickly and unappealing in certain lights. It can sometimes be hard to pinpoint accurately a chosen shade at the yellow end of the palette, as all the more troublesome properties of yellow may apply. The solution may be to break up surfaces and combine a variety of shades.

Green is best used like an orchestra, as a sum of parts rather than a stand-alone colour. It works best as part of a symphony, making its presence felt in separate but cohesive elements that include wood, texture and tone on tone. Think of all the greens in the garden or the forest and how lightweight leaves such as ferns reflect light through their tracery veins and become limey in tone, while thicker leaves and plants such as palms absorb the light and project deep racing green colours. Green is always a success combined with woody tones and wood itself, from pale ash or beech to warm oak, pine or wenge. Vivid shades of apple, pea, *Alchemilla mollis* and euphorbia both echo nature and create an instinctive complement to mocha and mahogany furniture or, indeed, brown painted walls. A green that veers towards the blue end of the story always warms walls

Green, like its constituent blue, is said to have a wider emotional range than red or yellow.

and makes an uplifting statement. It is best combined with plain or painted wood rather than used with busy patterned upholstery or fabric.

As a heritage colour, vivid pea green was a colour closely associated with the 18th and 19th centuries both in Europe and across the United States. At first it was only the wealthy who could afford to use strong colour, since the natural pigments used to create vivid paints were expensive and elusive. As cheaper formulations such as railing green and green verditer became available from the late 19th century onwards, so colour moved to a broader social spectrum. Many of these traditional greens had a blue bias and remain popular today, particularly in Swedish-style interiors, where traditional schemes have always favoured green-blues and blue-greens because they work well in limited northern light.

Green stands for growth, harmony and peaceful reassurance. Green in nature has texture, but can reproduce as a flat, cold tone on a wall. For warmth and depth, use a green that includes elements of burnt umber, red or yellow ochre.

In Art Deco interiors, mint greens were popular teamed with neapolitan ice cream shades of candy floss pink and noisette, while the Bloomsbury literary set in their Sussex enclave Charleston painted their rooms in many vivid hues, including a rich pea green. By the 1950s green had toned down and was more understated.

Nowadays, the subtle tones of olive, moss and khaki are finding favour with a generation for whom conservation and sustainable living are imperative. They team beautifully with fiery tangerine, sherbet lemon and jolts of fuchsia or gilt to make an enriching environment.

APPLE LIME

MINT TEA

SAGE GREEN

'Earthy greens are calm and soothing, ranging from the brighter realms of Farrow & Ball's "Churlish Green" to the perfect accent shades of "Ball Green" and "Vert de Terre". Greens have a natural affinity with earth colours, and provoke a pleasing counterpoint to soft lilac and muddy mauve tones.' SARAH COLE, DIRECTOR, FARROW & BALL

FOREST HILLS GREEN

FADED GREEN

CHAMELEON

USING GREEN What I call 'spiritual green', the clean tones of celadon and celery, are at once feminine, elusive and sophisticated. They add a subtle glamour wherever they are used but work particularly well in living rooms, bedrooms and bathrooms. Combined with off-whites and deep mocha, this shade is an unbeatable colour where you want to create a smart but subtle palette.

When choosing green palettes, make use of natural plants to help you fix on a particular shade. The garden greens of foliage and leaves are great starting points for formulating a wider palette. Pick sprigs of *Alchemilla mollis* or lily-of-the-valley to create a colour match for a no-nonsense range of leaf-inspired shades that are unmistakeably bright and breezy. Beware though that these richly textured organic forms can sometimes be hard to replicate in green paint, which can, like yellow, be tricky to handle. Make sure you choose a green that has a substantial amount of red, yellow ochre or burnt umber in its base. These shades will be warmer and deeper. If the tone of green is wrong it can affect your mood. An acidic green applied to kitchen or bathroom walls, for instance, will reflect badly on your face and make you look unhealthy.

Where there is a lot of light it is better to use blue-green or cool greens and where the light is grey and dark, chose warm greens. Dark greens are restful and meditative, perfect for a study or a library. They work well with orange-red, crimson brown and pink. Earthy greens look great with all browns. Think of how these tones work in nature when choosing shades to work with.

Green's opposite on the colour wheel is red and this vibrant juxtaposition conjures such delicious combinations as tomatoes and basil, rosy red apples and green leaves and fruits of the forest. Dirty greens and rich reds are a classic combination in traditional Swedish interiors, used on fabrics and painted furniture and woodwork, while Farrow & Ball's Cooking Apple Green is a lush, popular green that changes character according to light levels, becoming rich in sunlight and staying mellow in muted light.

It's best to experiment with understated greens before working up to bolder shades. Powerful greens on walls are capable of overpowering a space, whereas stronger tones on curtains and furnishings are less obtrusive.

Delicious accents for greens include rich russets teamed with sage green for subtle sophistication, and chocolate brown for a fashionable fix against faded lime or gentle pear. In living and dining areas greens are great for promoting relaxation and conversation, while in a kitchen pea green and salad shades are fresh and inviting, especially when combined with bright white, or buttercream for a slightly retro palette.

Using green as accents is particularly easy in kitchens and dining areas, where coloured glasses and deep green china are perennial favourites. Think red wine in green glasses and radicchio leaves on green plates; natural contrasts that provide table decoration in their own right. Complete the setting with green napkins and a wall painted in palest celery or celadon and the symphony will display all the right harmonies.

OPPOSITE TOP LEFT This pale apple snug area provides peaceful pause for thought in a Moroccan riad created by French designer Agnès Emery. She often uses tiles to produce colour, decoration, texture and interesting reflective surfaces in her energetic interiors.

OPPOSITE TOP RIGHT Exquisite celery green is at once elegant and enriching in this period dining room. Delicate accents are provided by chairs covered in toile de Jouy fabric, bone china edged in gold leaf and a cinnamon-coloured chandelier.

OPPOSITE BOTTOM Cool moss walls and a grey granite floor make a sophisticated statement, but shots of lemon yellow in cushions and decorative objects, plus fire and flame tones in a large rug bring the space to life.

Green has become an emblem for environmental awareness. It represents faith and immortality, is everlasting like mother nature and, of course, is the colour of the jungle, strong and reassuring.

avocado & pistachio | celery

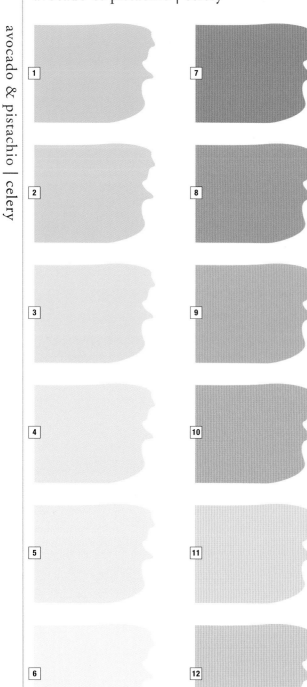

The green family is a happy and varied bunch of versatile shades, from palest celery to moody moss and olive via apple, mint and verdant leaf tones.

ABOVE Julie Prisca's 19th-century coaching inn in northern France has a pale but pretty palette. Icy green rough plaster walls, a hint of lavender and a good collection of jute and linen neutrals on upholstery create a soft coherence.

1 Springhill Green	**7** Gustavian Green
2 Lime Twist	**8** Spring Greens
3 Mint Tea	**9** Sage Green
4 Pine Sprigs	**10** Pine Tree
5 Chrome Green	**11** Mint Chocolate Chip
6 Pale Pear	**12** Chicory Tip

avocado & pistachio | apple

avocado & pistachio | apple

1
7
2
8
3
9
4
10
5
11
6
12

1 Apple Lime
2 Apple Orchard
3 Lime Grass
4 Bramley
5 Tasty Apple
6 Green Sherbet
7 Emerald
8 Jade
9 Mint Julep
10 Chameleon
11 Celadon
12 Cool Mint

avocado & pistachio | olive

avocado & pistachio | olive

1
7
2
8
3
9
4
10
5
11
6
12

1 Antique Green
2 Herb Garden
3 Forest Hills Green
4 Faded Green
5 Spring Valley
6 Fresh Dew
7 Deep Sea Green
8 Gothic Green
9 Willow Grove
10 Winchester Sage
11 Meadow
12 Dew

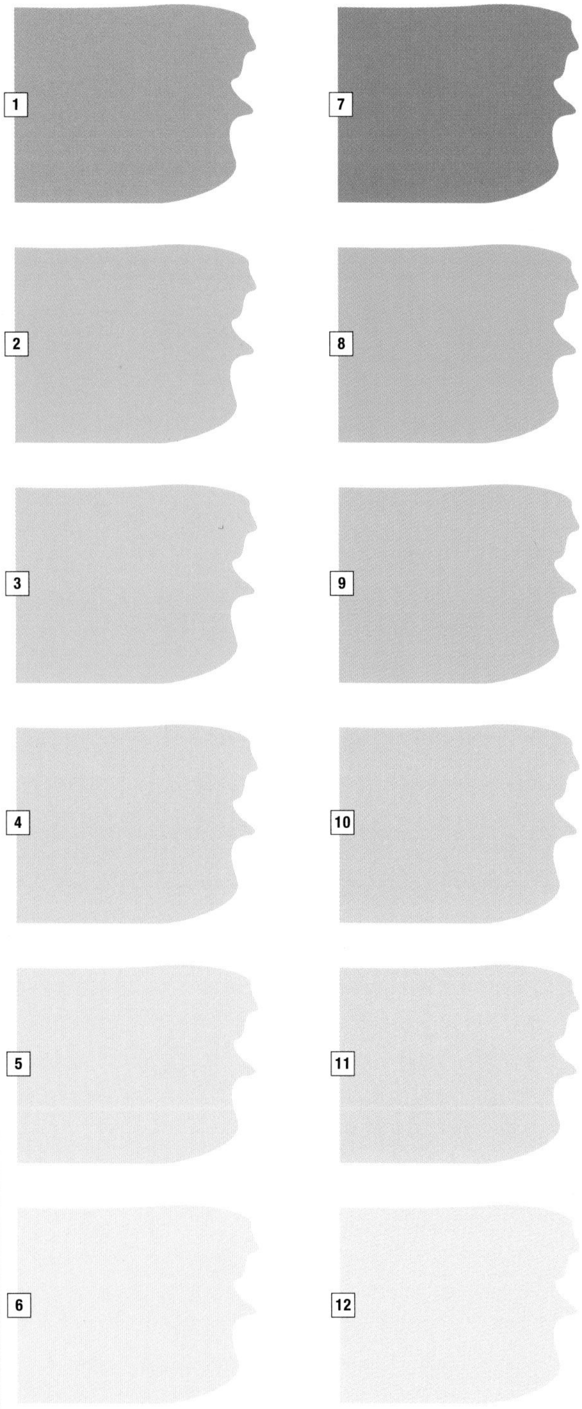

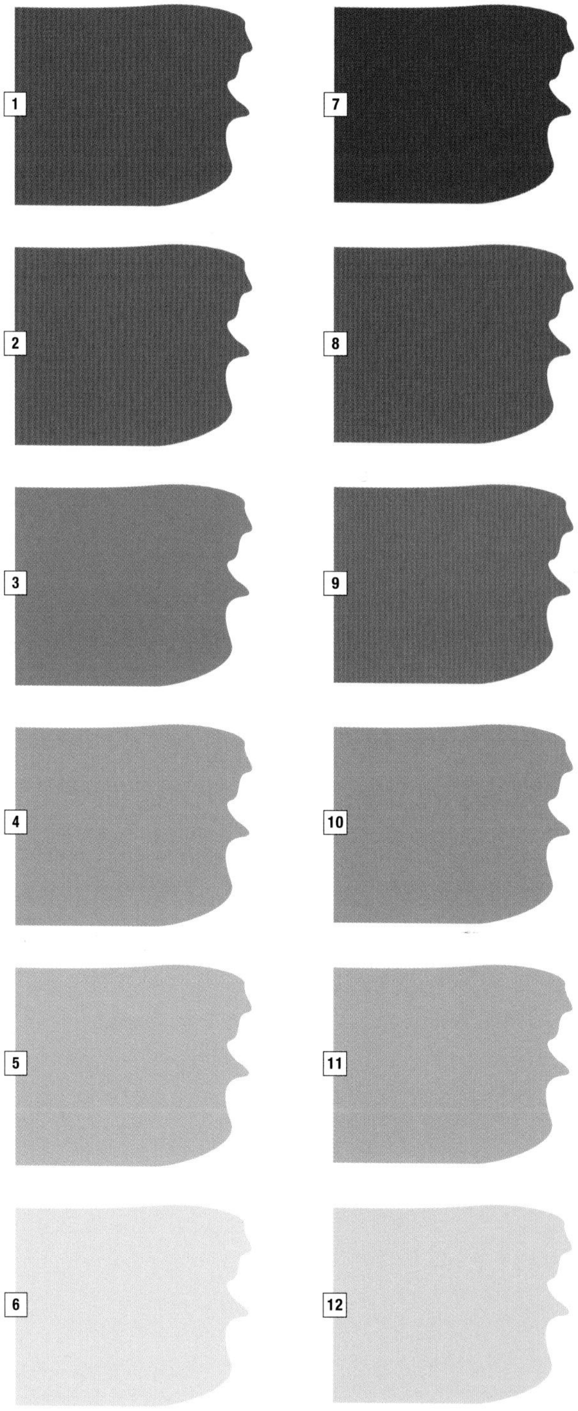

'Martha Stewart Signature's "Blue Hubbard 8053" is a modern pale blue tint, slightly neutral. In the north light in my living room, it is a soft grey-blue, but in warm west light, with lots of windows, it almost takes on a celadon cast as it does in my sister's house in Connecticut. The green grass and trees outside reflect a pale celadon cast.' ALEX BATES, WEST ELM

celery

THIS PAGE A floor-to-ceiling application of ethereal and calming soft mint allows abundant natural light to refract onto matt and gloss surfaces in a minimalist bedroom. This creates additional, dancing light in an empty but appealing space.

OPPOSITE Crisply feminine tones of palest celery and divine rosebud pink prove that using complementary shades on the colour wheel do not always have to produce a dramatic contrast, or be applied in violent hues.

At the delicate end of the green spectrum lie the leafy celery shades that are elegant, appealing and sometimes barely there. From palest celadon to Gustavian grey-greens and historical shades such as Farrow & Ball's pale greens, these classically understated tones work across a number of surfaces, from woodwork to walls and architectural detailing. Especially popular in the northern hemisphere are the sage green shades that take their cue from historic houses. These classic shades never lose their appeal and have been revived by Fine Paints of Europe in the US and Farrow & Ball on both sides of the Atlantic. Celery is always scrupulously smart for front doors as well as parlours, especially combined with deep racing green in a heritage combination and used on garden furniture and exterior woodwork as much as inside. These are colours that work best in matt rather than glossy finishes.

Grey-greens remind us of the colour of an olive leaf. These shades are usually not intense but soft, cool and muted. They work well with creams, browns and ochres, as well as royal blues and paler blues, especially when punctuated with deep browns and off-whites. Use slightly richer tones to combine with soft madder reds or pale rose for a classic complementary association that is fresh and uplifting. Such gentle associations work for guest rooms, living rooms and Swedish-style dining rooms. They are at their best when combined with muted shades of toning colours.

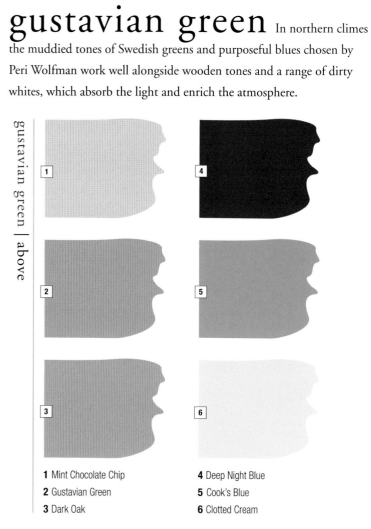

forest symphony
In a palette that combines grey-greens and shades of gilt and faded wood, this antiques-led living room by Lynn von Kersting evokes a woodland story, with soft fern tones, the gold of autumn leaves and bracken.

gustavian green
In northern climes the muddied tones of Swedish greens and purposeful blues chosen by Peri Wolfman work well alongside wooden tones and a range of dirty whites, which absorb the light and enrich the atmosphere.

forest symphony | above

1
2
3
4
5
6

1 Sage Green
2 Chicory Tip
3 White Truffle

4 Vienna Green
5 Caribbean Coast
6 Saffron

gustavian green | above

1
2
3
4
5
6

1 Mint Chocolate Chip
2 Gustavian Green
3 Dark Oak

4 Deep Night Blue
5 Cook's Blue
6 Clotted Cream

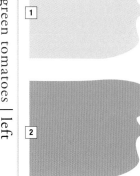

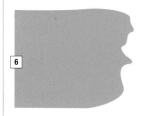

fried green tomatoes

Nature's palettes are always a source of inspiration. The delicious complementary shades of tomato red and apple orchard green refresh, revive and bring a sense of permanent summer to a cheerful bedroom, where the outdoors is not far away.

1 Sage Green
2 Spring Greens
3 Pelican Grey
4 Mother of Pearl
5 Ruby Red
6 Full Bloom

THIS PAGE Muted apple tones are a period classic, used in milky paints in New England.

OPPOSITE Snappy fresh apple in a hallway gives instant impact and a lively welcome.

'Apple tones are hugely versatile greens. Both warm and subtle, they steer a course between garden green and muted olive. Farrow & Ball's "Cooking Apple Green" works marvellously well in combination with "Pitch Blue" and off-whites to give a fresh, warming feel to kitchens and dining areas.' SARAH COLE, DIRECTOR, FARROW & BALL

apple

The true green of apples and the garden is at once clear and comforting. Perfect when combined with rich oak or pale ash and beech furniture, these tones provide a bright and reassuring backdrop given their associations with everything sustainable and wholesome. They work best when applied in a flat rather than glossy colour and are perfect for bedrooms, kitchens and dining areas or in spaces where concentration is required.

These apple greens, rather like lilacs, are capable of mutating throughout the day from pale apple to deep leaf green, so experiment with them on a piece of lining paper and observe the differing effects before committing to drenching a room in a colour you may not be sure about.

Apple shades work well with deep blues and bright whites as well as neutrals for a breezy, friendly palette, while complementary reds will provide sharp focus and more punch. They are quite strong tones in their own right and don't need too many distracting hues to accompany them, so keep the palette limited.

Exercise caution at the limey end of the scale. Sharp lime only really works on a small area as an accent in northern climes. It can look terrible in the cold light of the UK and northern Europe – not only too loud, but capable of draining the colour from your face, too, as light bounces away from it. Be sure not to let colours become too acidic, as this will push them too far towards an unflattering yellow.

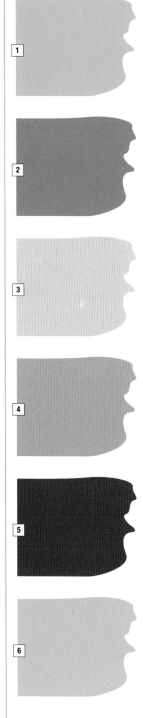

1 Mint Julep
2 Emerald
3 String
4 Dark Beige
5 Blazer Red
6 Fashion Pink

sage haven Muted greens are the most successful

of all for calming, comfortable living areas that are easy to spend time in.
Teamed with creamery whites and rose pink reds they make a palette of
soft complementary tones that are restful and not raucuous, and quite
different from a rich tomato red and a vivid leaf green.

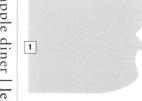

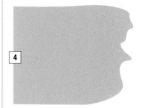

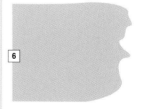

apple diner

On the tasteful side of the acid green spectrum, this lively apple green is one that mutates considerably according to the time of day. In the morning or in grey light, it can appear quite pale, but faced with bright sunlight or the full force of daytime, it will take on richer, deeper tones.

1 Bramley
2 Midnight Green
3 Paddington Blue
4 Blue Bayou
5 Natural White
6 Seed Pod

'Olive with all its infinite variations and blends is a striking colour, adding an unusual element to any space. With its transformative powers it has the ability to change the shape and size of a room from an ordinary one to something quite spectacular. It's soothing, calming, elegant and super glamorous.'

ABIGAIL AHERN, ATELIER ABIGAIL AHERN

olive

Cool khaki, mellow moss and safari greens comprise the olive scale, in which the more sombre but subtle greens reside. In colour preference tests men often prefer these muted shades to other brighter greens. Warm but considered, they are a good choice for smart living and dining areas, maybe less suited to bedrooms, but can be reassuring in work areas. They have an ability to remain muted in the background while still making a subliminal colour statement, versatile and enriching.

From almost taupe grey-greens to rich, deep moss via a brighter leaf green, this collection of shades is at the cooler end of the green spectrum. While green may be considered unlucky by some, it is a colour whose time is right, with the emphasis on renewal and sustainability at the forefront of every designer, and decorator's agenda. Sludgy greens in particular, which are infinitely versatile, are popular with decorators at the moment.

Good team players with olive are the autumnal shades of faded gold and deep russet taken from the complementary side of things, while analogous shades that sit well with them are cool taupes and browns, particularly the sandy beige almost neutral tones, as well as yellow ochre through to pale lemon tones and blues of any shade. Team them with shades of oatmeal and off-white rather than pure white, so that their subtlety is not stamped upon by too stark a contrast.

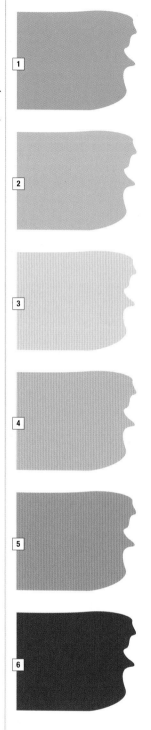

1 Faded Green
2 Pine Tree
3 Cornforth White
4 Beige Sand
5 Brassy Gold
6 London Burgundy

green mist In a David Collins' living room, smart
tones of creekland grey-greens, faded olive and deep bamboo conjure
morning mist and intriguing hues of barely there greens to produce a rich
but subtle palette that declares elegant comfort and is quite engrossing
in its inspired selection of elusive shades.

chinese green Designer David Carter

uses aged and distressed bottle-green walls as a backdrop for an ancient Chinese sign, quirky tasselled floor lamps and a vivid jade green table. These are deep, rich colours that definitely make a statement.

moroccan mix Designer Nathan

Turner's apartment is a Moroccan-inspired den where he combines ethnic-themed food with decoration in a palette of sharp gold tones with muted greens and rich reds against a backdrop of pearly off-white.

chinese green | above

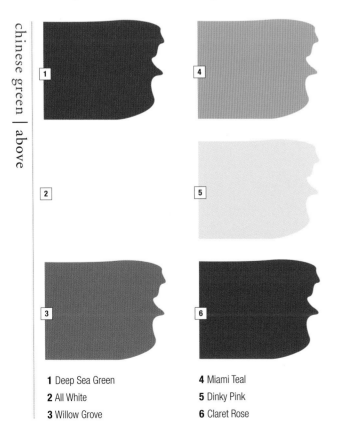

moroccan mix | above

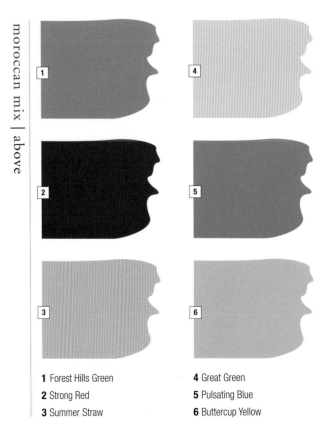

1 Deep Sea Green **4** Miami Teal

2 All White **5** Dinky Pink

3 Willow Grove **6** Claret Rose

1 Forest Hills Green **4** Great Green

2 Strong Red **5** Pulsating Blue

3 Summer Straw **6** Buttercup Yellow

earth
& clay

burnt sienna
papaya
putty
nutmeg
acorn
beeswax
ochre
polished plaster
pueblo
dark oak
allspice
brown sugar
oxblood
acacia honey
red fox
ginger
red brick
savannah
walnut
tan
mustard
mink
cracked wheat
paprika
santa fe
mud flat
terracotta
tupelo taupe
sable fur
noisette
mocha
mahogany
bitter chocolate
wenge

ALL ABOUT BROWN

Brown earth tones are natural shades often associated with their areas of provenance – Mexican adobe, Moroccan Kasbah colours, Scandinavian barn red or the coastal lime of west coast England. Never vivid or strong, the earth colours tend to be dark, gentle and cosy in outlook, always keeping the peace and offering a reassuring haven, wherever they appear.

Earth colours are never crude. They remind us of the natural pigments from which they are derived, such as raw or burnt umber, and are as popular with artists as they are with decorators. Earth tones are colours we respond to naturally and their warm tones work well with any light in any location. Perfect decorating tools indeed.

Just as browns of all shades are popular with fashion designers, they also influence and inspire many interior decorators, both contemporary and historical. Designers Kelly Hoppen, Michael Reeves and Jonathan Reed are all known for their use of luxurious tones of mole, beige and subtle spicy shades when creating fine, inviting spaces that shout class and elegance. The Bloomsbury set employed many shades of earth brown at their country retreat Charleston, in Sussex, while the Victorians were very fond of deep brown woodwork and earthy tones on fabrics and walls, as was William Morris, the arts and crafts designer. During the 1960s it seemed as though the earthy palettes containing rich shades of brown and orange were the only colours you could possibly consider decorating your home with, right down to mottled earthenware pottery for table settings and faded flame corduroy sofas being all the rage and seen everywhere.

Brown is the perfect diplomat – neither attention-seeking nor a shrinking violet, it is calm, steady and adaptable in any environment.

While brown was once considered ubiquitous and subsequently boring, it is in fact a deeply enriching colour whose wholesale revival has endured many changes of fashion within the interiors world, purely because of its versatility and emotional baggage. Think of the comfortable associations with a steaming cup of hot chocolate, the richly varied gleaming and glossy tones of dark espresso, the creamy textured finish of fudge or the fascinating patina of baked brownies.

Earth colours are timeless and organic, their naturally warm tones working well with any light and in any location. Use them in chalky finishes for an enveloping sense of wellbeing.

Surface and finish are most important when it comes to the brown palette. Wood is of course a vital element in earth-inspired palettes, its natural textures and variations providing additional depth to any brown story. A wooden floor, panelled walls or striking pieces of solid furniture are often used successfully as the main colour in an earth-inspired palette, together with a variety of basketware for additional textural interest. Wood combines well with analogous shades of brick red, smoky minks or cinnamon and cloves to complete the picture.

Key colours that also complement an earth palette include delicate shades of celery, celadon or apple at the subtle side of things or sharp yellows, topaz and burnt flame at the attention-grabbing end. The spicy tones of cinnamon and the more orange-earth colours combine well with Mediterranean sky blue, just as the buildings of a medina blend effortlessly with summer skies in a knocked-back version of the classic blue and orange complementary partnership. An equally good relationship is that of vivid swimming pool blue teamed with the colour of terracotta tiles.

MUD FLAT

'When used on exteriors, earthy tones make a home look like it is part of its environment, while they can be used indoors to create a warm, open and grounded atmosphere.' ANNE ROSSELT, PLASCON PAINTS

MOCHA EXPRESS

BROWN SUGAR

BEIGE SAND

TEXAS ROSE

SABLE FUR

CRACKED WHEAT

MILK CHOCOLATE

Chocolate notes, spicy flavours and the subtle tones of mole and adobe create happy combinations of earth colours that are scrupulously smart and richly defining.

USING BROWN Browns are perfect in spaces where warmth and comfort, simple luxury and fine backdrops are required. The paler tones of mole and plaster are ideal in rooms where you wish to place an emphasis on art pictures or delicate fabrics such as self-patterned silks or damasks, floaty sheers or nubbly textured fabrics such as linen, cord or cotton damask.

Combining tone-on-tone beige, taupe, pale chocolate and saffron, for instance, creates a wholesome story that is interesting but restful. These are tones that don't shout their presence, don't dominate the proceedings, but do provide an imperceptible sense of peace and proportion.

When working with these hues it is extremely important to use the right form of paint. Anything glossy or shiny will look unnatural and will reflect the light, making any space appear smaller. Instead use textured or matt paint to make the colour glow and add depth to the wall so it seems more natural and more spacious. Earthy palettes always work well on textured surfaces, so consider a rough plaster effect, either in physical form or by applying random layers of colour to ape a broken surface.

Keeping the ceiling white when you are applying earth colours to the walls will allow light to bounce from it and not draw attention to it, thereby making the room look higher.

Francesca Wezel has painted her drawing room a beautiful dark brown, using a limewash as a base. The room is exposed to the southwest and benefits from a good deal of natural light. During sunset the room lights up like a dream,

creating amazing tones that make you feel as though you are in a cosy, but not too dark, cave with an atmosphere that seems to hug and protect you. The surface looks like soft velvet and gives off a sense of wellbeing. Such tones are beautiful and will never date.

The middle-range of browns, in particular shades of toffee or toast, can be warm or cool, depending on their tone, but are definitely calm, subtle shades to work with. Caramel and cinnamon stories are well suited to creamy taupes and shades of oatmeal and pale butter.

In living rooms and bedrooms strong brown schemes often work well. Although the use of deep brown is a statement in itself, it is also perfectly complemented by splashes of vivid or pale turquoise and pink for a bolder finish. Introduce these accent colours by means of rugs, artwork, china and glass or cushions and throws.

Bathrooms, with their good supply of chrome surfaces, benefit from spots of brown in the form of pinky terracotta walls that provide warmth, not to mention flattering skin tones under artificial and natural light, while organic shades on walls, tiles and floors are enduringly popular.

At the richer end of the spectrum, definite browns are a natural choice for architectural detailing such as doors, panelling, dados, coving, cornicing and skirting. According to the strength of colour used, these elements will either clearly define a space, or, if kept pale and interesting, will become subtle framing elements. Rich browns on wooden floors or on panelling never fail to evoke a sense of solidity and warmth.

OPPOSITE TOP LEFT In the hallway of a period house, toffee and ochre tones combine in the patterned wallpaper, with glimpses of colourwashed walls in a study beyond.

OPPOSITE TOP RIGHT This Moroccan retreat designed by Studio KO of Paris is deliciously warmed by stonewashed tones applied directly to plaster walls.

OPPOSITE BOTTOM LEFT A faux suede bedhead in smart mole tones provides pleasing punctuation in a bedroom where dark wood and wheaten beige complete a subtle earthy palette.

OPPOSITE BOTTOM RIGHT A rich mix of linen, chenille, fur and velvet fabrics in mocha and chocolate shades sit perfectly against a wall painted in flat, chalky mud tones in this living room designed by Bernie de Le Cuona.

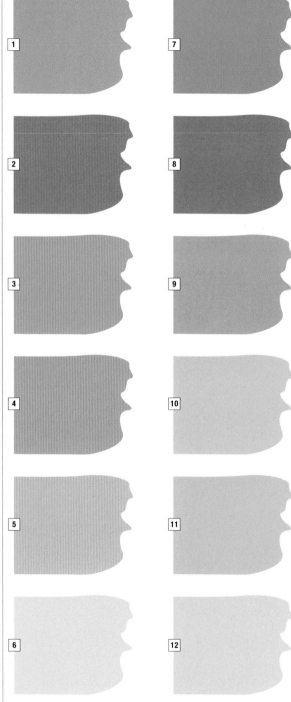

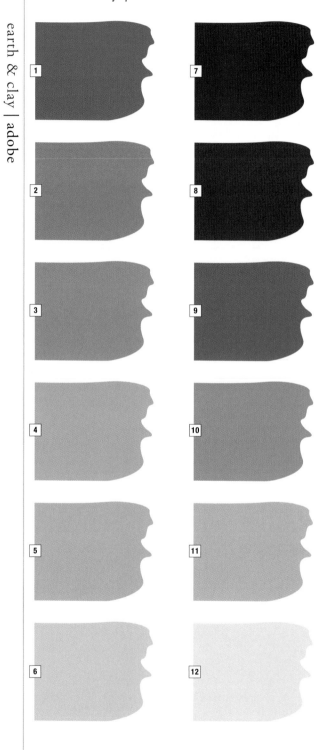

1 Santa Fe	**7** Burnt Sienna	**1** Milk Chocolate	**7** Oxblood
2 Allspice	**8** Orange Tan	**2** Noisette	**8** Boston Brick
3 Brown Sugar	**9** Saffron	**3** Mink	**9** Texas Rose
4 Mud Flat	**10** Beeswax	**4** Putty	**10** Polished Plaster
5 Ochre	**11** Acorn	**5** Milk Shake	**11** Pueblo
6 Oklahoma Wheat	**12** Ashbury Sand	**6** Pumice	**12** Fairest Pink

earth & clay | mole

earth & clay | chocolate

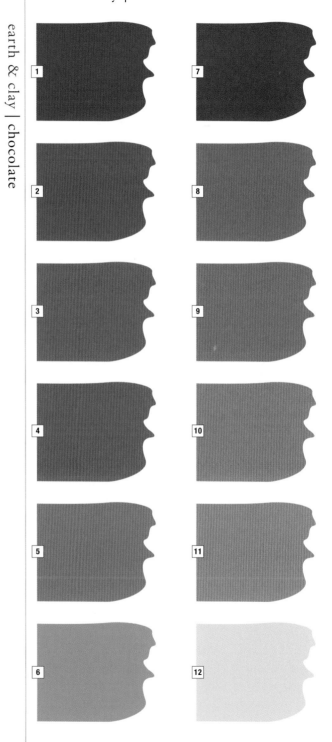

1 Taupetone	**7** Brownstone
2 Woodacres	**8** Café Crème
3 Sable Fur	**9** Raccoon Hollow
4 Tupelo Taupe	**10** Brandon Beige
5 Beige Sand	**11** French Linen
6 Chalk Pit	**12** Tapestry Beige

1 Cup O'Java	**7** Mahogany
2 Saddle Brown	**8** Mocha Express
3 Savannah	**9** Truffle
4 Bitter Chocolate	**10** Cracked Wheat
5 Dark Oak	**11** Smooth Pebble
6 Nutmeg	**12** Camel's Back

'Cinnamon tones have a wonderful rich quality. The burnt-orange undertone creates a warm, sociable, creative and friendly environment, perfect for a kitchen, dining room or living room. Cinnamon tones also look wonderful with wood, adding to the cosy ambience.' ANNE ROSSELT, PLASCON PAINTS

cinnamon

THIS PAGE Vibrant hot spice walls are defined and heightened by deep chocolate woodwork and detailing. Complementary blue accents in the form of small cups on the table may be small scale, but provide a jolt that makes the colours sing in this enriching, traditional dining space.

OPPOSITE Jamie Drake's masterful command of colour combines golden cinnamon tones in painted patchwork on the walls with soft turquoise green at the window in his New York apartment. Tonal variations on the spice theme create an enveloping sense of warmth.

Colourful cinnamon tones are perfectly suited to rooms with northern or cool light, such as the East Coast USA or northern Europe; as a collection of earth-toned colours warmed by yellow ochre, these warming colours work in all light levels. They instantly warm and embrace the space to make even the dingiest bedroom or living area come alive. Use cinnamon in varying tones such as saffron, brown sugar and nutmeg for a cohesive and interesting harmonious story. Add in a glossy sheen or additional texture on decorative accessories in the form of velvet cushions, silk throws or faux suede upholstery detailing for maximum effect and tone it down with deep, dark

shades of chocolate and ebony. Or you can contrast it with complementary soft muddy greens for a totally integrated palette that is at once rich and cosy.

Vibrant, spicy earth tones are traditionally associated with the locations where they are most often found. In particular they are found working their flavoursome magic in stunning exotic locations such as Morocco, Tuscany and Africa, where the sunny climate and generous natural light teases tonal treats from paintwork. In the desert of Arizona or the pueblos of New Mexico, the delicious hues of ginger, cumin and nutmeg create a richness that is grounding yet rich and bright. But don't be afraid to use this palette in less exotic situations as the hot, warm tones will still work, especially when teamed with other warm colours.

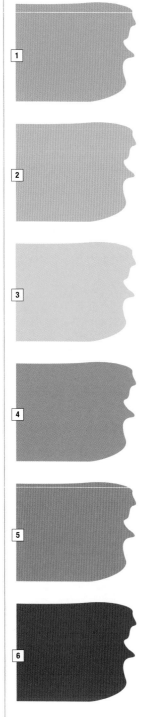

1 Brown Sugar
2 Beige Sand
3 Golden Yellow
4 Mandarin Fruit
5 Grey Suede
6 Leather

island spice New York designer Clodagh has
put together natural clove-coloured logs, soft washes of ochre on the walls
and a rich mix of spice tones on fabrics, floor and furnishings that team
with wall-mounted artwork for a superb exercise in colour combining
using analogous shades, from pale tangerine to cinnamon and saffron.

feeling the heat
In a Moroccan-inspired bedroom, deep chocolate browns anchor a scheme that relies on orange ochre walls and accents of russet for its colour. Sometimes subtle colour accents can provide a strong sense of colour in a room.

bathed in spice
Fabulously rich red colourwashed walls allow light to dance around a rustic bathroom in this Irish cottage. A lead bath bought from a Paris flea market provides more broken colour in a space that is dark but interesting.

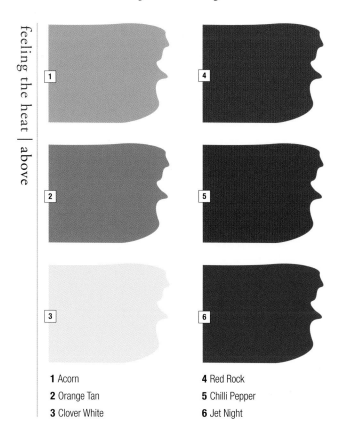

1

2

3

4

5

6

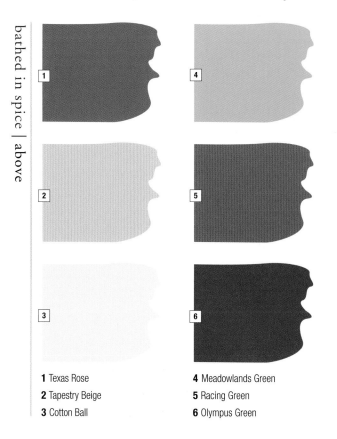

1

2

3

4

5

6

1 Acorn
2 Orange Tan
3 Clover White
4 Red Rock
5 Chilli Pepper
6 Jet Night

1 Texas Rose
2 Tapestry Beige
3 Cotton Ball
4 Meadowlands Green
5 Racing Green
6 Olympus Green

'These colours are never crude. They remind you of the earth, of the pigments from which they came. They are grounded, stable and secure and you can feel the relationship with their environment. Earthy tones are colours we respond naturally and warmly to. These colours work well with any light and in any location.' FRANCESCA WEZEL, FRANCESCA'S PAINTS

adobe

THIS PAGE Simply brimming with broken colour, these luscious toffee-toned walls conjure the warmth of adobe and the subtlety of a colourwash in a space that could lean towards the clinical were it not for these many interesting layers of texture.

OPPOSITE The adobe walls do the colour talking here. Fantastic painterly tones are a result of the earth, plaster and straw walls, designed to counteract the fierce Moroccan heat of this Corbusier-like house designed by Studio KO architects, Karl Fournier and Olivier Marty.

Adobe walls are found in the places where the sun beats strongly, such as southwestern USA and Africa, from Morocco to Yemen. The natural elements used in the formation of these thick, sometimes curved and uneven walls – earth, straw, clay and plaster among them – often perform the dual role of absorbing the heat of the sun during the day and radiating it away from the house during the night, to make sleeping more comfortable.

Materials used in adobe walls often influence the colour and style of the interior. Think of a Santa Fe pueblo building and its white, curved Mexican-style fireplace, which is both a focal point and an organic shape that may be echoed elsewhere in curved pieces of furniture. Adobe walls can be painted chalky white to help refract heat, but often their natural earthy hues are simply left to weather or are varnished to give the impression of a colourwashed wall, with interesting layers of broken colour forming on the uneven texture.

Classic adobe colours include red iron oxide, clay and straw, faded plaster pink and tones of mottled taupe. Studio KO architects, in their modern interpretation of adobe techniques, have created a fireplace in Marrakesh that dispenses with the curved organic form. It is clad in metal, follows the clean lines of contemporary design and combines richly textured natural walls with a floor of painted, varnished concrete. It is the adobe-style walls and an earthbound palette that create warmth.

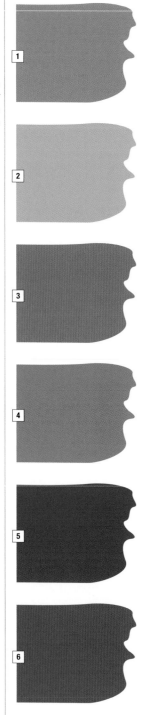

1 Noisette
2 Putty
3 Willow Grove
4 Orbit Glow
5 Hot Red
6 Vineyard

treetop cool South African architect Johann

Slee's forest 'treehouse' blurs the boundary of indoors and out. The interior space projects nature's palette back outdoors by means of complementary shades of leaf green and berry red. Enriching earth tones of rough plaster walls recreate the colour story found in the surrounding forest.

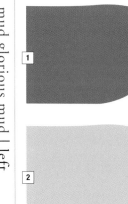

mud glorious mud

A symphony of browns is made interesting by combining plaster walls, distressed leather headboard and footboard on the bed and a glossy sheen on the polished woodwork. Punctuated with white bedlinen and cherry bedside tables with brass fittings, who said brown is boring?

1 Milk Chocolate
2 Pumice
3 All White
4 Hadley Red
5 Monticello Rose
6 Toasted Bean

'By layering varying tones, mole adds real depth to a room. Add textures, then the room really becomes alive: reflective steel, metallic fabrics, glass and lacquered surfaces add visual interest. Accent colours add a jolt and careful lighting should complement the colour tones, without detracting from the calm, tranquil feeling the colour mole emits.' MICHAEL REEVES

THIS PAGE A soothing mix of red brick, aged oak and elephant grey set off with a cool beige seat cushion is a sublime combination of subtle colours that are sympathetic and restful.

OPPOSITE Fabulously chic yet comfortable, these deep mole walls change shade by night, especially when lit by grandiose chandeliers formed from multiple empty bottles. Designer Virginia Fisher provides texture in the form of sisal matting, and elegant accents appear as artwork and on the upholstered dining chairs.

mole

The mole shades are the tasteful taupes of the earth palette, the chic and sophisticated neutral-leaning shades that encompass the red-tinged browns of camel and mushroom, together with the soft, interesting textural beauty of suede and linen, faux fur and leather.

Mole can be sharp and sophisticated when used as a palette of toning shades. Rich, subtle and astoundingly elegant, these shades work well when displaying their natural affinity with the other stronger earth colours, as part of a palette that combines shades such as spice and saffron, red brick and mocha teamed with pale neutrals such as grey, toasted oats or latte. Mole shades may also shine when defined and rendered smart by black detailing or accented with suggestions of the warm reds that form part of their base colour.

Straddling the boundary of earth tones, the night and day shades and even straying into pannacotta and cappuccino, what keeps these colours down to earth is their inherent cool, brown nature. They work beautifully when emphasized with unusual accents such as flame, burnt ginger, Chinese reds or sharp lime greens. Natural colours such as vanilla and clotted cream work well with this palette, as do natural textures such as limestone, linen, glass and granite. Warm, welcoming and a provider of reassuring tones, mole can be wonderfully utilized in rooms such as living areas and bedrooms where comfort is key.

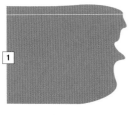
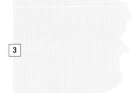
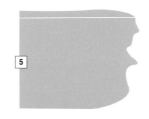

silver grey

Multiple metallic surfaces combine with the clear clay walls to make a sophisticated colour statement, punctuated with black and white. Accents of green provided by foliage and flowers make a neat counterpoint to the neutral tones used elsewhere in the space on the walls, floor and the furnishing fabrics.

1 Tupelo Taupe
2 Shadow Grey
3 Cloudy Grey
4 Cotton Ball
5 Grass
6 Jungle

1
2
3
4
5
6

fired earth The colour brown is formed from

a mix of black and red in varying proportions, which is why brown
and red and black and red make such excellent colour companions.
This palette of reds, orange-browns and deep taupe walls is an
interesting and lively interpretation of a brown story.

1 Sable Fur
2 Flax
3 Savoury Cream
4 Pumpkin Spice
5 Shy Cherry
6 Misty Morning

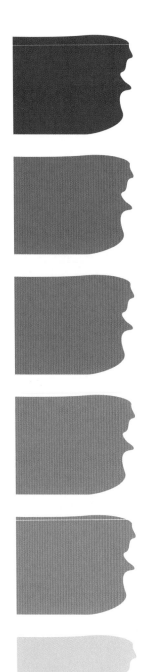

'Rich, deep chocolate tones are both grounding and reassuring. Serious but warming, they both complement and highlight neutral tones. Colours of nature such as muddy greens, buttermilk tones and off-white shades combine beautifully with earthy oranges and steely blues.' ANN GRAFTON,

MANAGING DIRECTOR OF GP & J BAKER

THIS PAGE Designer Bernie de Le Cuona includes a fluid flash of analogous orange for a subtle take on the classic red and brown combination. Russet, cherrywood, jute and cocoa all add to the delicious mix.

OPPOSITE Chocolate walls, the bedframe and bedside furniture are the perfect counterpoint to white walls and curtains, softened with an indigo blue bedcover, in this smart and sophisticated bedroom designed by Ilaria Miani.

chocolate

Chocolate is a hip and happening palette, since it made a dramatic comeback in the early 21st century as a serious colour to use in the home. Hot chocolate is the colour of dark wood and delicious treats, sleek and sophisticated, capable of appearing smart and contemporary or creating a traditional polished effect. Or think of the toffee and caramel tones of animal fur, where tone-on-tone chocolate, butterscotch and liquorice combine in a mellifluous brown haze to denote soft comfort.

From the rich, smooth and glossy bittersweet tones of deepest ebony to the matt, chalky and opaque finish of limed oak, or the cocoa dust hues of chocolate truffles, chocolate-coloured walls or floors may be treated so as to be reflective and refined or dirtied up, to create a more informal appearance. Matt and chalky paints give depth to a room and make it look bigger, so in a small space, experiment with these types of paint finishes for an enlarging effect.

Floors are the place where chocolate tones never fail to anchor a colour scheme and provide dark definition. When used on walls, too, the deeply dark ambience that emerges benefits from accent colours to brighten the effect. Vivid turquoise, lemon sherbet and baby blue provide exciting tonal variations to lift such a scheme and prevent an overly masculine feel. Chocolate colours are formed by a mix of red and black, so it's no surprise that red with chocolate is a comfortable choice.

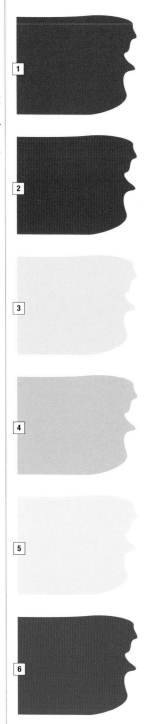

1 Mahogany
2 Salsa
3 Café Latte
4 Glimmer
5 Citronee
6 Seaport Blue

topaz & toffee Jewel-bright accents on

cushions, flowers and accessories bring vivid life to this living room by
designer Philip Gorrivan. The whole colour balance in a room can be
shifted by adding or subtracting bright cushions, pictures and mirrors to or
from a space. Topaz and turquoise are especially good foils for dark colours.

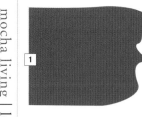

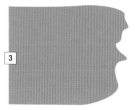

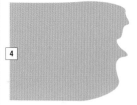

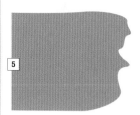

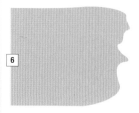

mocha living It is texture that is important in this tone-on-tone amalgamation of polished oak and linen. Alternate walls were lined with cherry panelling and painted in bitter chocolate by 20th-century architect Patrick Gwynne. A symphony of browns, from the orange end of the spectrum to the rich and moody chocolate, predominate.

1 Cup O'Java
2 Saddle Brown
3 Forest Green
4 Antique Brown
5 Deep Gilt
6 Mouse Grey

night
& day

titanium white
chanel chic
nautical white
egyptian cotton
arctic fox
tundra ice
mother of pearl
polar bear
china cup
chalk
ice blue
silver birch
stainless steel
silver
chrome
gunmetal
pearl
gustavian grey
black truffle
jet
blackcurrant jelly
liquorice
aniline black
carbon
black ash
blackboard
dove
grey ash
elephant grey
night sky
squid ink
pewter
charcoal
graphite

ALL ABOUT MONOCHROME

The monochrome tones are indispensable decorating tools, whether creating a simple black and white room or using them to define, punctuate or neutralize a colour scheme. The jury is out over whether black is a colour, since an object will look black when all the wavelengths of the light spectrum are absorbed in its surface. Strictly speaking, black and white perform like light reflectors and absorbers rather than containing particular pigments or being borne out of two or more other definite colours.

It is easy to dismiss black and white as an 'easy' palette to work with, or even a predictable one. In fact it is a classic complementary partnership, graphic, clean and scrupulously elegant, and capable of being at once bold and understated. Think of the classic Chanel graphics and the couture clothes, cowhide, zebra stripes, the endless possibilities of black type on white paper. All of them are perfectly chic and astoundingly smart.

Black is a smart definer and surprisingly unobtrusive as an accent colour when it appears on architectural details such as panelling, worktops, slate fireplaces, floors and ceiling beams. Blacks tinted with blue provide a more reflective surface, while those at the grey end of the spectrum have a smoky tint that is seldom less than chic.

Pure white can be incredibly cold and grey if used in the wrong tones. The ice whites or pure whites will always need to be warmed by other, richer shades if they are not going to bathe a room in a dull cast. But white as a decorating colour choice encourages a clear mind, de-clutters the senses and allows creative thought free rein. It provides a pure backdrop that enables us to create fresh and inviting spaces.

Grey, the median interloper between black and white, is chic and elegant. It is one of my favourite shades and I am fascinated by its endless versatility. Certainly not dull and boring, its crisp clean tones are capable of harnessing the best light from many other colours, throwing them all into perfect balance. Be inspired by the soft metallic sheen of an Armani suit or brushed steel, and how light bounces effortlessly off such surfaces to give a pleasing sheen. Grey is the perfect mixer, flattering all the other colours and allowing them to shine and be at their best.

Within this supposedly predictable palette are many other nuances on this far from narrow spectrum. The silvery greys, the fragile alabaster shades, the glamorous metallic shades of silver and the smoky slate tones graduate towards midnight tones, deep reflective anthracite and, eventually, black.

> Black, white and grey are the 'colourless' shades that are cool, smart and endlessly adaptable. They work best in chic bedrooms, classic living areas and contemporary kitchens.

Some rooms, where the colour balance is directed to black as the dominant colour, are considered urban masculine spaces – this look is particularly associated with large bedrooms or kitchens where you find a lot of stainless steel hardware. Treat black in a room the same way as you would a little black dress and accessorize to your heart's content. Silver, reds, greens and yellows, whether in vivid primary tones or knocked-back shades, all work with the dark neutral tones of black. In rooms where black is an important element in the colour palette, it will look more striking when used in matt, chalky tones on the walls. On furniture, black looks at its best when applied in a glossy finish, for a look that is at once sleek and sophisticated.

Black is a powerful shade, and too much of it can bathe a room in dark and disturbing mystery that is uncomfortable to live with, rather than a dramatic cast, so keep its importance in proportion.

'Monochromatic is the easiest scheme to achieve as it is based on one colour which is adjusted by adding white to lighten or black to darken, producing a tint or shade respectively.' DAVID OLIVER, THE PAINT LIBRARY

STAINLESS STEEL

SNOW WHITE

PEWTER

BLACKBOARD

WHITE ICE

AIRFORCE BLUE

Black is a colour with a permanent backstage pass when it comes to room design. Always there in the wings, not stealing the limelight, but an indispensable part of any successful colour palette.

USING MONOCHROME Rooms that are predominantly decorated in white, grey or black all benefit from accent colours, rich textures or tone-on-tone layers of these shades to really bring them alive and provide an alternative colour focus. For accent colours choose from deep coral reds, faded lime greens, sharp turquoise or bitter yellows for jolts of bright shades that are strong but not overpowering.

Stacked logs against white walls in a living room or dining space lend a warming texture to black and white spaces and hint at a Danish modern style, ever popular for urban apartments and simple, contemporary country rooms. The whites in these spaces should be chosen with care, so as not to make any black tones act as a strong coolant in the space. If you use whites with a small amount of red or yellow ochre in them this will warm them through.

The mid-tone greys of flannel, pewter and seal is where grey is pushed towards the brown end of the spectrum. This whole browny-white spectrum mixes really well with harmonious earth colours such as bone, mushroom and all shades of brown. Layer these colours tone on tone for a marvellously cohesive palette that lends itself to any room of the house, but is particularly restful for living rooms and bedrooms.

Mid-tone greys work wonderfully well on woodwork and can be surprising in their smartness. Although often dismissed as cold or dull, they are superb in combination with other monochrome shades, teamed with cool white furniture and smart steely greys. Texture, in the form of fabrics such as checked or striped grey-toned tweeds, boiled wool or roughly woven linens always adds depth to a plain scheme. For a warm grey, choose one that incorporates a dash of beige to take away any chilly tones.

Grey as a colour is capable of looking both stylish and completely cosy, from contemporary urban settings to informal rural retreats. It is a shade that is versatile and under-rated. Use it as a warm, mellow evening colour, or as a crisp daytime definer. Set it to work on walls or woodwork and enjoy its smart tones as a key part of a palette rather than as a throwaway accent.

Rich, dark greys, the colour of anthracite and slate, are enriching tones that go with everything. They are especially good winter warming colours that complement white. Such a combination will give you a smart palette that is chic and urban in style. Be sure to apply wall colour in a matt finish, then add layers of gloss or sheen by means of mirrors, crystal or glass. Or paint wooden furniture in gloss tones for a sense of luxury.

Use black for defining details: as an edging on picture frames, piping on furniture and punctuation around windows and on doors in the form of curtain poles and door furniture. When it does take centre stage it provides deep drama, especially when mixed with reflective surfaces such as mirror and steel.

The classic black and white story is always at home in a bathroom, where clean white walls team well with black and white tiles on walls and floors. The same can be said for a kitchen, where this palette gives an American retro feel.

night & day | snow

night & day | metallic grey

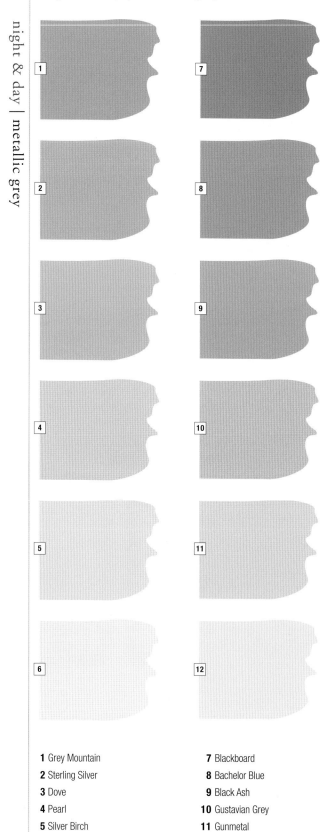

1 Nautical White	**7** White Ice	**1** Grey Mountain	**7** Blackboard
2 Arctic Fox	**8** Polar Bear	**2** Sterling Silver	**8** Bachelor Blue
3 China Cup	**9** Tundra Ice	**3** Dove	**9** Black Ash
4 Egyptian Cotton	**10** Winter Snow	**4** Pearl	**10** Gustavian Grey
5 Chalk	**11** Titanium White	**5** Silver Birch	**11** Gunmetal
6 Mother of Pearl	**12** Snow White	**6** Chrome	**12** Stainless Steel

The monochrome shades of black, white and grey may lack strong colour, but certainly pack a dramatic punch, whether used over large areas or as intriguing detailing in a space – perfect partners not sleeping partners.

BELOW Black and ebony detailing on an ironwork bedframe and curtain pole, in addition to dark brown basketware and mahogany chairs, provides crisp definition in an otherwise soft white bedroom.

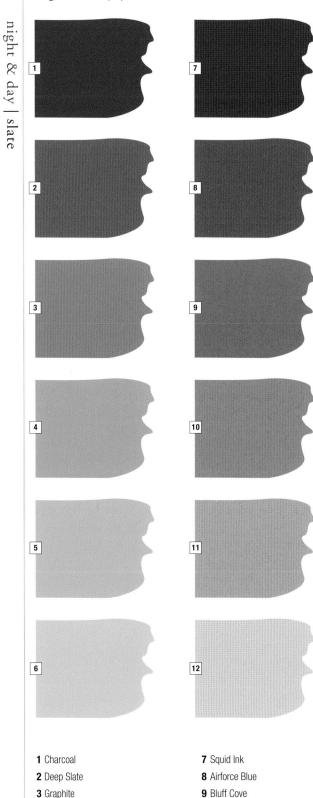

1 Charcoal	7 Squid Ink
2 Deep Slate	8 Airforce Blue
3 Graphite	9 Bluff Cove
4 Elephant Grey	10 Silver Mink
5 Pewter	11 Ice Blue
6 Pelican Grey	12 Grey Ash

'Why choose white? Because it is anything but dull and predictable. It creates light, opens up space and provides a perfect backdrop for other tones and textures. My favourites shades are whites with a slight touch of green to them. Somehow they are clean and fresh without ever feeling cold.' ATLANTA BARTLETT, STYLIST, PALE AND INTERESTING

snow

Titanium white is perhaps the perfect snow colour. Pure white is mixed with a touch of black to produce an almost imperceptible grey tinge that produces a pure, slightly cool white. Such a cool colour needs to be warmed by other colours for it to succeed in a colour palette. Combine it with rich reds, browny greens (rather than yellow-greens, which will make it seem even colder) and regal blues for a crisp nautical edge. And soften it with slate grey boiled wool throws, wood-framed furniture or a selection of interesting black and white accessories such as framed photographs, or steel-based lamps or curtain poles.

Pure white walls can be stylish but need careful handling. Brilliant white can turn out to be just as difficult to work with as yellow, so be prepared to introduce warm and enriching colours to accompany it, especially in an already grey northern light. Whereas brilliant white walls in a Greek island retreat will sing with cheer, they will actually throw a grey cast over proceedings in a London terraced house or New York loft. The trick is in the mix and ensuring the right level of purity. When it is right, pure white is invigorating and refreshing. Try incorporating a variety of whites for a warmer finish. Stick to a warm white on the ceiling and cooler whites on woodwork and detailing. Many designers revel in all-white living spaces, as they provide a blank canvas in which they can consider other concepts without too much visual distraction.

THIS PAGE This is a glorious example of the pure beauty that a monochrome palette is capable of producing. It is all about using the right combination of warm whites, slate and midnight black, accented with oatmeal, pale grey and splashes of texture.

OPPOSITE Bluff white shutters and walls provide a serene backdrop in a period living room, where red and white ticking cushions are a crisp counterpoint.

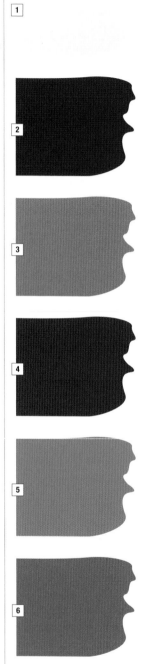

1 Jute
2 Charcoal
3 Forest Hills Green
4 Turkish Coffee
5 Bronzed Brown
6 Walled Garden

lofty whites

Vicente Wolf designs New York lofts like no one else. This impeccably sophisticated space combines simple styling and intriguing amounts of forest and khaki shades set against brown and taupe fabrics. The antique grey walls and ceiling and limestone-tiled floor form an unobtrusive backdrop that allows the furniture to speak.

white wood In an all-white room it is

important to vary the whites and introduce splashes of colour to break up the space. Jolts of lilac and turquoise counterpoint the sage green and white chequerboard floor in this bright and breezy dining area. A combination of whites is a clean and uplifting palette, as long as you choose carefully.

1 Mother of Pearl
2 Pale Pear
3 Yukon Sky
4 Tupelo Green
5 Cayman Blue
6 Passion Plum

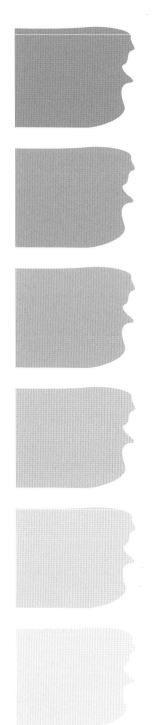

'Metallic finishes will reflect light and bring life to matt surfaces. I love creating layers of interesting textures and often use steely dark greys and jet black mixed with delicate, dirty off-whites to create smart, flattering spaces.' DOMINIQUE KIEFFER

metallic grey

The shimmering tones of metallic finishes such as silver, bronze, crystal, steel and glass have graduated from interesting adjuncts to centre stage in many contemporary colour schemes. Rich, interesting tones are being created by many designers, including Michael Reeves and Kelly Hoppen, with a sensitive use of gloss that, used in the right proportion and on the right surfaces, provides glamour rather than glitz, taste rather than tack.

The neutral elegance of metallic tones provides a glow that enhances classic palettes such as the grey, weathered look of Scandinavian interiors or French country Provençal schemes at the traditional end of things. At the contemporary cutting edge, silvery walls provide a sharp backdrop for oversized mirrors, statement crystal chandeliers and satin fabrics.

From the pearl grey shades of zinc to pale silver leaf, sophisticated grey tones look amazing on woodwork and work too as definition on furniture, picture frames and mirrors. Metallic grey and steel work well hand in hand with indigo or slightly knocked-back fuchsia accents for a smart and understated colour story.

To make sure grey tones are warm, add a dash of beige to remove any lingering cool tones. Pearl grey is a good mellow evening colour and is capable of working well in urban or country settings. Used on floors, reflective glossy greys make a perfect lively anchor for a combination of monochrome tones.

deco shimmer

The combination of reflective surfaces and very appealing colourwashed and glazed walls, mixed with deep, white-painted period panelling and touches of deep claret, produce a smart, updated 1930s colour palette.

deco shimmer | opposite

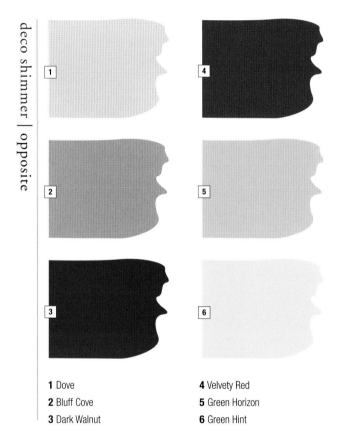

1 Dove

2 Bluff Cove

3 Dark Walnut

4 Velvety Red

5 Green Horizon

6 Green Hint

Reflective surfaces add a fascinating dimension to the metallic colours of gunmetal, steel and cosy grey. Combine metallic paint with glossy furniture for the most vivid effect.

pewter perfection

A grey symphony of pewter-toned woodwork and walls treated with a glaze of metallic paint echoes traditional Swedish style, with painted furniture using colours that are cool enough to ape an ice house yet also retain an element of warmth and welcome.

pewter perfection | above

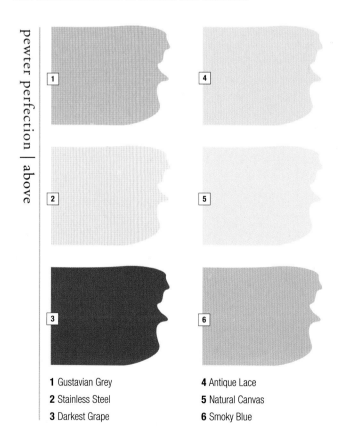

1 Gustavian Grey

2 Stainless Steel

3 Darkest Grape

4 Antique Lace

5 Natural Canvas

6 Smoky Blue

'Combining black with white may not seem an obvious pairing, but it throws up smart, chic solutions when placed alongside harmonious shades of white and grey and punctuated with shots of colour. I love the clarity produced by these sharp, clear tones.' JOHN BARMAN

THIS PAGE At the charcoal end of the grey spectrum, these painted stair risers and skirting give graphic definition to a curved staircase, creating an architectural statement in a tall hallway.

OPPOSITE A graphite-inspired bedroom mixes a masculine palette with chrome styling and a contemporary colourful wall panel by Kelly Stuart Graham.

slate

Although dark, moody greys and near blacks are colours that are perhaps more associated with incidental elements in a palette, used on painted floors, as detailing on picture frames and furniture edging, they are in fact quite stunning used as a main colour in a room too. Combine them with white, rich woody tones and paler greys or steely blues and ochre for a sleek, smart palette that works in a number of settings, from cool, urban retro chic to classic, pared-down country style or traditional interiors.

Midnight black and blue are powerful tones in their own right so are best softened with shots of other colours, while deep slate greys are perfect with whites for schemes that are reminiscent of felted blankets and welcoming sheets.

Slate floors are particularly successful paired with creams and sage greens or used as foils for black architectural features in a room with paler neutrals. Other colours that harmonize well with a deep grey/black story include oxblood, celadon, moody grey-blues and a richer Shaker blue. Keep any blues and greens muted rather than bright for the most sophisticated combinations, and use the citric shades of lemon and lime, or fuchsia and orange, for a more complementary approach. Tone-on-tone combinations are best approached by using elements of all the Night & Day shades. Use metallic surfaces in the form of chandeliers, mirrors or chrome-edged furniture with luxurious velvet or satin throws in delicious greys and indulge in jet woodwork.

tropical glamour
An edgy mauve on a rough concrete wall is perfectly counterpointed with ebony gloss floorboards, deep grey woodwork, a black metal bedframe and a grey-tiled sunken bath in a palette that is ultra smart for a bedroom.

black notes
Frank Faulkner's conglomeration of a high-gloss white floor and ice grey walls is a classical, and very successful, interpretation of the monochrome theme. Several black accents are present in the form of furniture and accessories.

tropical glamour | above

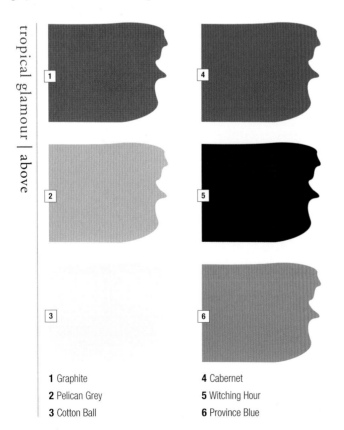

black notes | above

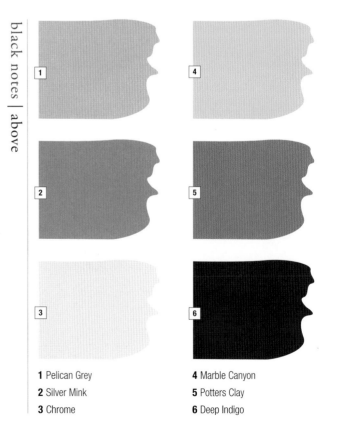

1 Graphite

2 Pelican Grey

3 Cotton Ball

4 Cabernet

5 Witching Hour

6 Province Blue

1 Pelican Grey

2 Silver Mink

3 Chrome

4 Marble Canyon

5 Potters Clay

6 Deep Indigo

fine dining
Midnight oil walls are framed by designer Alexandra Champalimaud with flat-painted architraving and built-in cabinetry, inset with marbled panelling and skirting. They make a rich and textured counterpoint to the dark wood, leather-bound dining chairs and glossy wood on the table and the floor.

1 Charcoal
2 Lantern Light
3 Clotted Cream
4 Deep Ocean Blue
5 Hollow Brown
6 Moleskin

northern lights
Black-painted kitchen units are the only dark shades against white walls and eaves in Peri Wolfman's country kitchen. An aged butcher's block and a stripped floor provide an element of visual warmth in the monochrome space.

total tar
In Normandy, designer Dominique Kieffer's utility room combines deep grey, tar and white for a serious-looking, practical space. The draped linen conceals white appliances while clean linen is stored in a seed chest painted deep elephant grey.

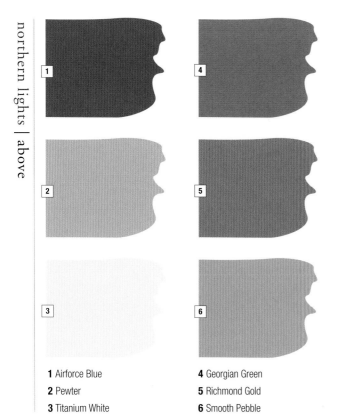

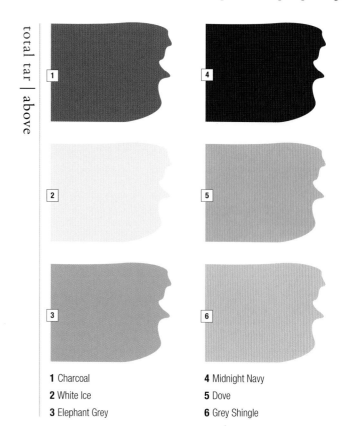

1 Airforce Blue

2 Pewter

3 Titanium White

4 Georgian Green

5 Richmond Gold

6 Smooth Pebble

1 Charcoal

2 White Ice

3 Elephant Grey

4 Midnight Navy

5 Dove

6 Grey Shingle

green & black
Kristiina Ratia uses greenery to accent and enliven clean monochromes in a screened outdoor room where natural light is in abundance. Plants bring the outside in as well as helping to refresh the pale scheme.

safari plains
Gentle olive and beige tones on walls and floor are neatly framed by designer Jeffrey Bilhuber with white woodwork. An oversized panelled door painted in deep elephant grey makes a majestic statement, counterpointed by flanking chairs.

green & black | above

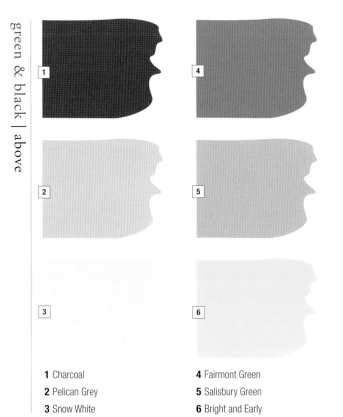

safari plains | above

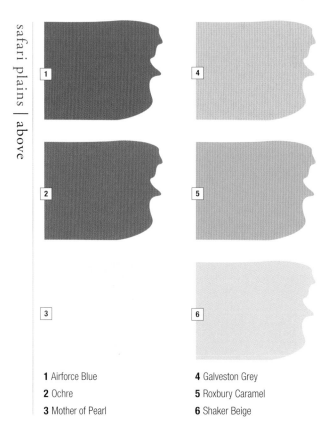

1 Charcoal

2 Pelican Grey

3 Snow White

4 Fairmont Green

5 Salisbury Green

6 Bright and Early

1 Airforce Blue

2 Ochre

3 Mother of Pearl

4 Galveston Grey

5 Roxbury Caramel

6 Shaker Beige

pannacotta
& cappuccino

crème brûlée
cotton ball
string
jute
oatmeal
mascarpone
ivory
porcelain
vanilla
café latte
dairy milk
cornish cream
clotted cream
popcorn
sesame seed
cashmere
bleached beech
caramel
bone
barley
mimosa
butterscotch
natural canvas
papyrus
orchid
raw silk
limewash
calla lily
white hyacinth
alabaster
white truffle
madeira cake
wheatgrass
lily of the valley

ALL ABOUT OFF-WHITES

From barely there off-whites to buttermilk, butterscotch and biscotti, the off-white neutral tones are the holy grail of colour palettes for me; they are soothing tones that are never out of date. Combine them with any number of similar and harmonious tones and you will never be disappointed, as they look beautiful under most lights and create palettes that are wonderfully warming and comfortable. They have the ability to work particularly well in contemporary spaces, yet never look out of place in pared-down country homes.

Nearly all decorators cite a particular off-white among their personal favourites in any little black book of decorating secrets. When it comes to creating cool but calm interiors, these are undemanding yet stunning colours. Relatively easy to choose and widely available, they are popular to work with. They are among the colours I truly love to live and decorate with, and I simply revel in their understated elegance.

Off-white, like black, performs differently from other colours in the way that it reflects and absorbs light. White will reflect almost all other colours, so be aware of this when choosing colours to go with it. You may not want a pale yellow, for instance, to be projected across a room and cast unflattering lights. If you are in a cold northern light, it is best to choose an off-white that contains a higher proportion of raw umber for a subtle fawn or taupe colour slant.

Creating a palette with such divine, elusive shades is both a pleasure and a challenge. The uninitiated may think 'Surely off-white is just dirty white?' Wrong. There are at least as many shades of white and off-white as there are days in a year, and some innovative paint companies, including David Oliver's the Paint Library and Farrow & Ball, have created their own palettes consisting solely of off-whites. They have sourced and refined a useful collection of subtle shades that are suitable for many different, colour-tinged neutral stories from shades that mix white with tinges of grey, brown, red, green and blue. These are the shades that are more readily mixed into white to provide the richer, warmer off-whites.

Getting the white right is important if you want a room to be warm and welcoming rather than drab with a grey cast. When you look around any paint shop you will realize just how many shades of off-white there are and how each one has its own subtle colour balance within it. Gather together a collection of different off-white palettes and get used to looking at off-whites as colours within colours. This way you can quickly identify which palette they have a natural affinity with.

The most useful 'dirty whites' often have a tiny element of raw umber in their base. This is a natural brown clay pigment that provides a beige cast to pure white paint. Grey-whites are achieved by combining white with a stronger element of deeper umber, while an increase in both elements will result in a mole colour.

There is a reason why the once dreadfully ubiquitous magnolia was as popular as it was. It was tinged with a particularly warm yellow ochre that made a room welcoming but inoffensive, neutral but bland. Warmer neutrals are the biscotti and buttermilk shades that include hints of yellow and brown, while cool neutrals include the pure whites of ricotta verging on the grey-green. These welcoming shades, combined with black and white and textured tones of toffee and gilt, have a still serenity to them, in a carefully chosen tableau of colours that create delicious harmony and an easy smartness.

The perfect off-whites step on the toes of true colours, but don't intrude into definite colour statements. From cow's milk to cappuccino, they provide nuance rather than drama, notes rather than a full symphony.

ALABASTER

BUTTER CHURN

'From palest porcelain to light latte
the off-whites never fail to provoke
a serene sense of calm and harmony.
Easy to live with, subtle to work
with, use them wherever you need a
smart, cohesive but relaxed palette.'

ATLANTA BARTLETT, STYLIST, PALE AND INTERESTING

NATURAL CANVAS

CAFÉ LATTE

LILY OF THE VALLEY

BLEACHED BEECH

USING OFF-WHITES Off-whites are everywhere, sometimes noticeable, sometimes blending into the background of a space where stronger colours take centre stage. It's hard to go wrong when experimenting with and combining these gentle shades of linen, string and latte, but layering them tone on tone, from the palest to the darkest, will add visual interest. Effortlessly elegant, they are versatile shades that can be kept subtle or enlivened with striking accent colours.

Natural surfaces are the perfect companions to these shades. Wood, stone, glass and granite are all materials that provide texture, pattern and deeper neutral shades in an off-white scheme. But beware, because sometimes so many natural tones in one space can look a bit bland if they are piled one on top of another in haphazard fashion. Make sure to choose maybe three or four base colours and use them on a variety of surfaces for the best effect. Use fabrics that echo an architectural feature, or match the wall colour with accessories such as rugs and throws.

Adding in rich but subtle accent earth colours such as Pompeii red, terracotta and cocoa are the sensible deeper-toned companions for the base palette. To add some vigour to the palette, throw in some turquoise or shots of lime. Floors are important in an all-white scheme. Wooden floors – whether natural oak boards, a deep nut-brown painted floor or boards painted in a white colourwash or limed – are the perfect anchor for white spaces. Experiment with gloss surfaces or deep, light-absorbing paint colours to provide additional texture and sheen.

Off-whites work in almost every room of the house, but are particularly smart in living rooms, bedrooms and bathrooms, where their neutral elegance allows furniture, bedlinen or chrome detailing to add extra layers of texture and

From the barely there tones of ricotta and mascarpone to the richer dairy shades of buttermilk and cappuccino, off-whites are the warm neutrals that never fail to create a welcome.

colour to a scheme. Use them in gloss form on woodwork and floors for a crisp sheen in a totally white space or to provide glamorous definition where walls are in quite strong colours.

Off-whites are as perfectly at home in small spaces, where they blur the boundaries of confining walls, as they are in generous, light-filled rooms, where they infuse the space with an ethereal quality. In small spaces keep to one white or off-white. In larger spaces you can use a variety of whites and introduce a number of natural textures, too, for a layered approach. Use a number of different off-white shades on doors, windows and architectural detailing, then introduce shades of, say, linen, jute and string across a number of surfaces such as rugs, upholstery, cushions and throws.

When choosing colours to accompany off-whites, remember that adding white to a pure shade will produce a tint that lightens the overall colour, so this is a good way to create a colour you know will be sympathetic to the off-white. Adding grey to a pure hue changes the base colour to a grey-toned version of it, for instance a pale grey mole rather than chocolate brown or pale pinky beige. In this way you can manipulate the stronger colours in a room so that they complement the off-whites.

Whichever neutral direction you choose to go in, keep the base colours mixed with an essentially warm shade and you can't go wrong.

OPPOSITE TOP LEFT In an Helsinki apartment full of cold northern light, a careful choice of rose-tinged whites and a sleek glossy floor make this white space warm despite its location.

OPPOSITE TOP RIGHT Cool alabaster white walls are framed with an intricate stonework mantle and hearth. Animal prints in black and white and a nubbly rug soften the room but continue the palette.

OPPOSITE BOTTOM LEFT In Connecticut, designer Jeffrey Bilhuber lets the natural light become part of a breezy bleached white story. There is nothing so inspiring as the perfect off-white.

OPPOSITE BOTTOM RIGHT In this Atlanta living room, designed by Tim Hobby of Space, Tim has made delicate use of ivory, vanilla ice and biscuit shades to create an enchanting, understated glamour.

pannacotta & cappuccino | ricotta

pannacotta & cappuccino | buttermilk

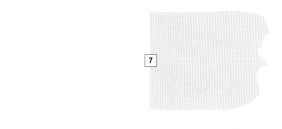

pannacotta & cappuccino | ricotta

pannacotta & cappuccino | buttermilk

1 Cotton Ball	7 Jute
2 Orchid	8 String
3 Clotted Cream	9 Oatmeal
4 Mother of Pearl	10 Natural Canvas
5 Alabaster	11 Bone
6 Calla Lily	12 Mimosa

1 Papyrus	7 Crème Brûlée
2 Curd	8 Sesame Seed
3 Cow's Milk	9 Salmon White
4 Popcorn	10 Ambrosia
5 Lily of the Valley	11 Warm Blush
6 Vanilla	12 Butter Churn

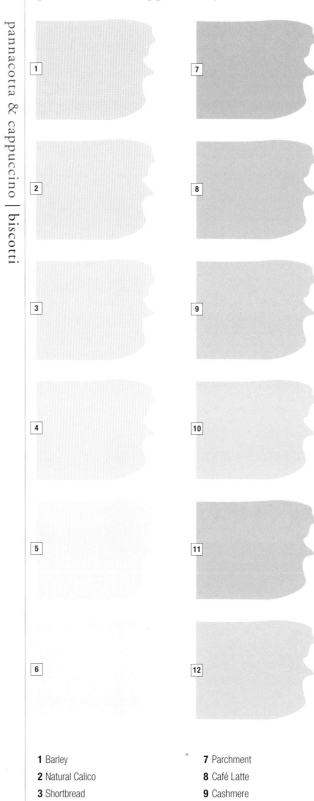

Neutrals are the perfect colours to decorate with. Calm, sophisticated and always reassuring, they are capable of providing a subtle backdrop or of taking central casting by storm.

ABOVE Creamy wall tones of buttermilk provide a warming neutral backdrop for accent tones of faded coral and muted reds.

1 Barley
2 Natural Calico
3 Shortbread
4 Cornish Cream
5 White Truffle
6 Dairy Milk

7 Parchment
8 Café Latte
9 Cashmere
10 Bleached Beech
11 Oat Cake
12 Limewash

'To me the perfect white is very neutral, like my favourite, Benjamin Moore's "Super White". I like whites that give space a sense of architecture without decorating it. A pure, untainted white creates the best plain canvas that I can create my rooms against.' VICENTE WOLF

ricotta

Put a barely there off-white next to a pure brilliant white, especially under a natural light source, and you will be amazed at the difference in tone. What can be described as white in a bright Mediterranean light can look almost grey in cold northern light, so it is important to get the white right before you cover a room with it. The pale whites of ricotta and mascarpone, bone white and white truffle are great 'pale dairy' colours that are oh-so-subtle yet bathe a space in warm, natural light. Combine them in matt and gloss finishes for a perfect neutral marriage that allows surfaces to interact with one another and lets the light dance around a room. These pale milky whites make good

accent colours on woodwork and furniture for stronger shades in a room. Team bone whites with weathered greys, faded greens, rosy reds, pale lilacs or strong blues for the best effect. They will both highlight the colours and provide delicate definition. Introduce texture in the form of sisal matting, loose linen covers and glossy woodwork, on walls or floors, to add further levels of visual interest.

Or bathe a whole room in porcelain tones for an all-white story that is surprisingly restful, particularly when accented with black detailing or touches of warm wood. Barely there whites can be both restful but smart, informal but elegant. Use them in kitchens for a clean, fresh look, in living rooms where a level of understated elegance is required or in a bedroom with a sunny aspect.

spring colours

Rich ricotta walls are simply stunning in company with palest celadon, sunflower and lemon yellow and Swedish blue. A fresh, invigorating palette, this is one that is impossible to tire of, whatever the season.

1 Clotted Cream

2 Chalk Pit

3 Pewter

4 Yellow Flower

5 Billowy Down

6 Cactus Flower

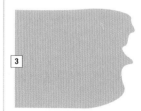

lilac linen
An urban London home is bathed in light thanks to warm ricotta tones that are varied by one or two shades on walls, woodwork and cornicing. Textured sisal flooring in natural colours and honey-coloured incidental furniture mix well with lilac linen on the cushions and neutral furnishings.

1 Alabaster
2 Clotted Cream
3 Beige Sand
4 Lavender Blue
5 Wild Orchid
6 Exotic Red

'I like obsessive continuity in colour. I paint walls, ceilings and woodwork all the same in matt paint and high skirtings the same colour in gloss. I prefer off-white colours.' MIMMI O'CONNELL

buttermilk

The creamy tones of buttermilk, from soft wheat to crème brûlée, have faint tinges of yellow. These are in fact browny tones formed by varying intensities of the natural yellow ochre pigment that lends the colour value. The resultant colour is a warm off-white that never looks stark, even in northern light. These warm dairy shades of butter, ivory and creamy milk work wonderfully well with rich oak tones, shades of royal blue and ochre-sand tones. Schemes can be pushed towards a Provençal and Mediterranean feel, a muted take on a red and white theme or else a traditional and enduring food-inspired chocolate and cream palette. Buttermilk and deep brown  is a pleasing and reassuring palette that is endlessly versatile for kitchens, living areas and bedrooms, or indeed any room where natural materials and colours are present. Deep corals and faded reds also look splendid with these tones – think peaches and cream. Navy blues conjure the nautical, while celery greens mixed with buttery tones create a sense of nature. Combine them with other neutrals such as earthy moles and taupes, wax-candle dairy shades and spicy cinnamon or ginger tones.

Buttermilk shades add depth, so use them in spaces where an enveloping feel is required, in kitchens and bedrooms, for instance. Particularly suited to the northern hemisphere, they perform the same function there as pure white in sunnier places, providing a perfect backdrop against which stronger colours can perform.

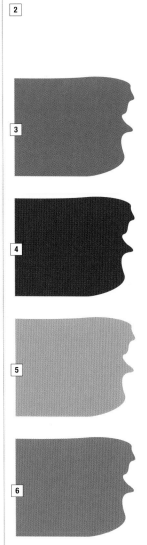

strawberries & cream

A palette comprising a wall colour that could be magnolia by another name provides a calming backdrop for off-white three-quarter panelled walls and seating. Elements of strawberry crush on the rug underfoot, cushions and curtain detailing lend interest and impact to the room.

1 Curd
2 Winter Snow
3 Dark Oak
4 Deep Rose
5 Mauve Mist
6 Mauve Sable

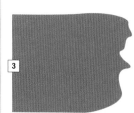

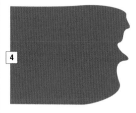

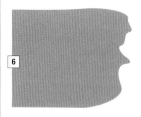

buttercup & mole This neutral

story embraces the smudgy browns of felled trees, stormy skies and rich buttermilk in the patterned curtains and picked up elsewhere in the room. These balanced tones create a fresh and natural scheme that works as well for the country as it would for the coast.

1 Lily of the Valley
2 Stoneground
3 Allspice
4 Blueberry
5 Paper White
6 French Horn

'No colour works in isolation, and finding a new combination of colours that look wonderful together can be both rewarding and exciting. A subtle variation of colour is an effective way of uniting all the architectural elements of a room, which are frequently painted white through habit or un-adventure.' DAVID OLIVER, THE PAINT LIBRARY

THIS PAGE Faded ice cream colours make perfect partners for oaten walls. These soft neutrals are both fresh and fetching in a quaint, period scullery kitchen decorated with creamware serving platters.

OPPOSITE A marvellous array of wheat, biscuit and beige gives this bedroom a smart, airy feel. Distressed paintwork on the wardrobe and a pleasing textured window blind add layers of interest to the palette.

biscotti

These caramel-toned neutrals are the stalwarts of the pannacotta palette, capable of being accessorized to make a grand statement, or of acting alone in an elegant class of their own. Versatile but never boring, they are a clear asset in rooms where natural light is limited, providing a neutral but not dull palette. Embolden these wheaten shades with dashes of lacquer red or jungle green to bring attention to them, or use harmonious tones of taupe, butterscotch, camel and cappuccino for a toffee-tinged space. These deeper neutral tones are often tinted with browns and pinks that give them their natural warmth and allow colours other than pure latte to emanate from

their surfaces. Natural surfaces and fabrics such as velvet, suede, leather and animal skins are perfectly at home in this colour range. For accents introduce elements of honey tones in the shape of brass lampstands, gilt mirrors or candlesticks and caramel-tinged sheepskin for layers of texture and reflective surfaces. Delicate, pale china in creamy tones of palest primrose and faded rose have their colours accented and enhanced by biscotti shades, particularly when applied to walls as a colourwash.

Biscotti colours work well in any room, but always provide a crisp edge in bathrooms, living rooms, bedrooms and hallways. Their raw umber-edged tones work in any kind of light and in any style of interior, whether country or contemporary, in a limited or a generous space.

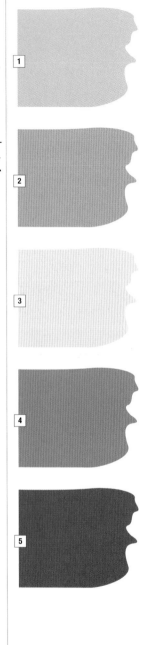

1 Parchment
2 Golden Wheat
3 Green Pearl
4 Field Green
5 Mocha Express
6 Pale Primrose

cappuccino screen A single

feature wall in cappuccino tones breaks up a multi-purpose space of cool linen colours, screening the staircase and becoming a focal point in the colour scheme too. A floor-to-ceiling statement picked out in this way also provides the illusion of additional height.

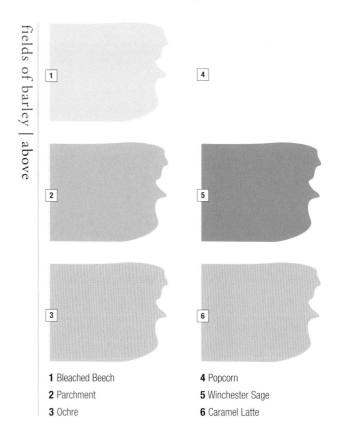

fade to grey

This bedroom designed by Luigi Esposito combines a simple black and white palette for the furniture and bedlinen with a delightful faux-suede wall in toasty jute tones. Its broken texture softens the darker black plains in the room.

fields of barley

A combination of delicate stripes, checks and florals, clotted cream woodwork and toffee notes is easy on the eye, creating a soft and welcoming atmosphere. These glorious tones succeed in being luxurious but still informal.

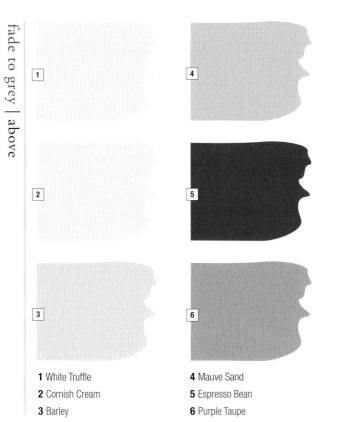

fade to grey | above

1

4

2

5

3

6

1 White Truffle

2 Cornish Cream

3 Barley

4 Mauve Sand

5 Espresso Bean

6 Purple Taupe

fields of barley | above

1

4

2

5

3

6

1 Bleached Beech

2 Parchment

3 Ochre

4 Popcorn

5 Winchester Sage

6 Caramel Latte

Sources for paint colours

SEA & SKY

PAGE 83
Mexico Dulux 93BG 32/374; Crown Paints True Blue 20 E 51 **Aquamarine** Dulux 50BG 30/384; Crown Historic Paints Q9.20.56 **Poolside** Dulux 70BG 32/238; Francesca's Paints Giorgio's Wisteria **Cobalt** Dulux 31BB 23/340; Crown Paints RAL 5015 **Gunmetal Blue** Flamant SE308 Myrtille; Dulux 30BB 17/158 **Military Uniform** Fired Earth Bamiyan Blue 89; Flamant 151 Copenhagen Blue

PAGE 86 SUMMER SKIES
1 Mexico Dulux 93BG 32/374; Crown Paints True Blue 20 E 51 **2 Kingfisher** Dulux 70BG 40/284; Homebase Marine Blue **3 Forget-me-Not** Dulux 79BG 53/259; Fired Earth Welkin Blue 87 **4 Rockpool** Dulux 74BG 61/206; Homebase Azure **5 Wedgwood** Dulux 46BG 63/190; Homebase Lazy Blue **6 Delft** Dulux 50BG 72/170; Crown Paints Historic Colours M5.04.80 **7 Aquamarine** Dulux 50BG 30/384; Crown Historic Paints Q9.20.56 **8 Beach Shack** Dulux 30BG 33/269; Little Greene Paint Company Polar Blue 121 **9 Turquoise** Dulux 30BG 44/248; Crown Paints Historic Colours P7.13.67 **10 Shoreline** Dulux 48BG 54/244; Fired Earth Duck Egg 99 **11 Grey Day** Dulux 13BG 72/151; Fired Earth Northern Lights 98 **12 Duck Egg** Dulux 10BG 72/092; Little Greene Paint Company Gentle Sky 102

PAGE 87 OCEAN
1 Prussian Blue Farrow & Ball Pitch Blue 220; Dulux 50BB 11/321 **2 Cobalt** Dulux 31BB 23/340; Crown Paints RAL 5015 **3 Periwinkle** Dulux 16BB 41/268; Crown Paints Historic Colours S2.19.62 **4 Faded Denim** Dulux 70BG 53/164; Sanderson Gown Blue 26-22M **5 Cool Blue** Dulux 66BG 68/157; Fired Earth Blue Ashes 92 **6 Ice Blue** Dulux 50BG 76/079; Francesca's Paints Water Green II **7 Midnight Sky** Dulux 70BG 10/214; Crown Paints Cosmos 18 C 39 **8 Shaker Blue** Dulux 70BG 16/209; Crown Paints Historic Colours R5.28.43 **9 Poolside** Dulux 70BG 32/238; Francesca's Paints Giorgio's Wisteria **10 Cabina** Dulux 70BG 41/201; Little Greene Paint Company Blue Verditer 104 **11 Athenian Blue** Dulux 70BG 47/182; Little Greene Paint Company Sky Blue 103 **12 Hawaiian Breeze** Dulux 50BG 62/133; Sanderson Coverlet 28-9P

PAGE 87 STORMY
1 Midnight Blue Farrow & Ball Hague Blue 30; Dulux 70BG 07/086 **2 Moonlight** Dulux 10BB 09/155; Flamant SE312 Abysse **3 Deep Navy** Dulux 30BB 10/112; Flamant P94 Blue Jeans **4 Pebble Grey** Dulux 10BB 18/106; Crown Paints Historic Colours RO.07.47 **5 Steely Sky** Dulux 70BG 28/060; Flamant 170 Baleine **6 Wedgwood Grey** Sanderson Blue Clay 45-4M; Flamant 159 Iode **7 Evening Sky** Dulux 50BB 10/112; Flamant 152 Bleu de Toi **8 Gunmetal Blue** Flamant SE308 Myrtille; Dulux 30BB 17/158 **9 Military Uniform** Fired Earth Bamiyan Blue 89; Flamant 151 Copenhagen Blue **10 Harlequin Blue** Dulux 30BB 32/139; Sanderson Zenith Blue 88 **11 Gustavian** Dulux 30BB 46/124; Francesca's Paints Spanish Blue **12 Blue-Grey** Dulux 90BG 63/072; Fired Earth Glass Samphire 91

PAGE 90 RICH WOOD
1 Wedgwood Dulux 46BG 63/190; Homebase Lazy Blue **2 Plaster Pink** Francesca's Paints Dawn Warning; Sanderson Sangaree 17-23M **3 Snow White** Dulux 30GY 88/014; Crown Historic Paints G8.03.88 **4 Walnut Tan** Dulux 90YR 18/177; Crown Historic Paints C9.08.39 **5 Light Ochre** Dulux 30YY 64/331; Crown Historic Paints F8.25.79 **6 Meadow Barley** Dulux 10YY 76/084; Crown Historic Paints F2.06.82

PAGE 90 MANHATTAN COOL
1 Shoreline Dulux 48BG 54/244; Fired Earth Duck Egg 99 **2 Cool Blue** Dulux 66BG 68/157; Fired Earth Blue Ashes 92 **3 Dirty White** Farrow & Ball Blackened 201; Fired Earth Platinum Pale 2 **4 Florida Green** Dulux 02GG 21/542; Crown Historic Paints L5.20.48 **5 Springhill Green** Dulux 33GY 46/469; Flamant 179 Bambou **6 Princess Pink** Dulux 95RB 56/237; Nutshell Natural Paints 113CAS5

PAGE 91 PROVENCAL DINING
1 Rockpool Dulux 74BG 61/206; Homebase Azure **2 Kingfisher** Dulux 70BG 40/284; Homebase Marine Blue **3 Blue-Grey** Dulux 90BG 63/072; Fired Earth Glass Samphire 91 **4 Ladybird Red** Dulux 10YR 15/500; Paint & Paper Library Very Well Read **5 Genuine Pink** Dulux 70RR 38/246; Fired Earth Rose Bay 76 **6 Moroccan Red** Dulux 26YR 30/511; Crown Paints Colorado 04 E 51

PAGE 93 CHINA CORNER
1 Delft Dulux 50BG 72/170; Crown Paints Historic Colours M5.04.80 **2 Gustavian** Dulux 30BB 46/124; Francesca's Paints Spanish Blue **3 Periwinkle** Dulux 16BB 41/268; Crown Paints Historic Colours S2.19.62 **4 Cobalt** Dulux 31BB 23/340; Crown Paints RAL 5015 **5 Butter Churn** Fired Earth Marble 43; Dulux 20YY 83/063 **6 Winchester Sage** Farrow & Ball Folly Green 76; Francesca's Paints Lucia's Apple Green

PAGE 93 COASTAL CALM
1 Wedgwood Dulux 46BG 63/190; Homebase Lazy Blue **2 Harlequin Blue** Dulux 30BB 32/139; Sanderson Zenith Blue 88 **3 Cashmere** Dulux 40YY 72/164; Farrow & Ball String 8 **4 Dove Wing** Francesca's Paints Peace White; Paint & Paper Library Sand I **5 Vermilion** Dulux 16YR 18/587; Fired Earth Cochineal 65 **6 Marine Blue** Farrow & Ball Drawing Room Blue 253; Dulux 10BB 07/150

PAGE 96 SPANISH MODERN
1 Prussian Blue Farrow & Ball Pitch Blue 220; Dulux 50BB 11/321 **2 Winter Gates** Farrow & Ball Hardwick White; Flamant P43 Digue **3 Silver Birch** Dulux 00YY 63/024; Little Greene Paint Company Welcome 109 **4 Secluded Beach** Farrow & Ball Farrow's Cream; Fired Earth Roman Ochre 62 **5 Noisette** Dulux 70YR 35/216; Paint & Paper Library Tudor Rose **6 Classic Brown** Dulux 70YR 07/093; Flamant 198 Tartuffo

PAGE 97 TURQUOISE TWIST
1 Athenian Blue Dulux 70BG 47/182; Little Greene Paint Company Sky Blue 103 **2 Delft** Dulux 50BG 72/170; Crown Paints Historic Colours M5.04.80 **3 Ochre** Little Greene Paint Company Straw Colour 44; Nutshell Natural Paints 107CA55 Cinnamon 5 **4 Great White** Farrow & Ball Great White 2006; Francesca's Paints Elephant II **5 Greenfield Pumpkin** Dulux 00YY 18/346; Little Greene Paint Company Stone-Park-Warm 36 **6 Roxbury Caramel** Dulux 20YY 49/271; Farrow & Ball Dutch Pink 62

PAGE 100 WEDGWOOD BLUES
1 Gunmetal Blue Flamant SE308 Myrtille; Dulux 30BB 17/158 **2 Gunmetal** Dulux 50BG 64/028; Francesca's Paints Hibiscus Blue **3 Silver Birch** Dulux 00YY 63/024; Little Greene Paint Company Welcome 109 **4 Plum Pie** Dulux 70RB 23/203; Francesca's Paints Piedmontese Aubergine **5 Ansonia Peach** Dulux 80YR 55/266; Francesca's Paints Mixed Pepper **6 Titanium White** Dulux 98YY 82/022; Francesca's Paints Emperor's Marble

PAGE 101 GREY SKIES
1 Harlequin Blue Dulux 30BB 32/139; Sanderson Zenith Blue 88 **2 Blue-Grey** Dulux 90BG 63/072; Fired Earth Glass Samphire 91 **3 Graphite** Dulux 30BB 31/043;Little Greene Mid Lead Colour 114 **4 Cord** Farrow & Ball Cord 16; Dulux 20YY 57/178 **5 Blueberry** SE326 Opera; Farrow & Ball Pelt 254 **6 Violet Petal** Francesca's Paints Lavender I; Flamant JU406 Chwing Gum

PAGE 101 COOL CUISINE
1 Military Uniform Fired Earth Bamiyan Blue 89; Flamant 151 Copenhagen Blue **2 Gustavian Grey** Dulux 90BG 48/057; Farrow & Ball Parma Gray 27 **3 Pueblo** Flamant 181 Blush; Dulux 10YR 67/111 **4 Mother of Pearl** Paint & Paper Library Sand I; Farrow & Ball James White 2010 **5 Pitch Blue** Farrow & Ball Pitch Blue 220; Dulux 30BB 18/190 **6 Summer Sunshine** Farrow & Ball Print Room Yellow 69; Paint & Paper Library Othman Brae

AVOCADO & PISTACHIO

PAGE 105
Apple Lime Dulux 34GY 40/515; Crown Paints RAL 6018 **Forest Hills Green** Little Greene Paint Company Garden 86; Flamant 192 Petit Pois **Mint Tea** Dulux 30GY 72/196; Crown Paints Pale Green **Faded Green** Francesca's Paints Casa Bruciata's Muddy Green; Flamant SE309 Pastis **Sage Green** Francesca's Paints Mint III; Fired Earth Summer Lichen 109 **Chameleon** Dulux 9GY 76/158; Crown Paints Cool Aqua

PAGE 108 CELERY
1 Springhill Green Dulux 33GY 46/469; Flamant 179 Bambou **2 Lime Twist** Dulux 30GY 58/375; Crown Historic Colours H3.29.65 **3 Mint Tea** Dulux 30GY 72/196; Crown Paints Pale Green **4 Pine Sprigs** Dulux 30GY 75/251; Crown Paints RAL 6019 **5 Chrome Green** Dulux 30GY 72/196; Sanderson Olive Mist 41-9P **6 Pale Pear** Dulux 30GY 83/107; Crown Historic Colours J0.08.80 **7 Gustavian Green** Francesca's Paints Casa Bruciata's Muddy Green; Crown Paints Peridot 12 B 21 **8 Spring Greens** Farrow & Ball Saxon Green 80; Snderson Willow Vale 39-22M **9 Sage Green** Francesca's Paints Mint III; Fired Earth Summer Lichen 109 **10 Pine Tree** Farrow & Ball Cooking Apple Green 32; Little Greene Paint Company Kitchen Green 85 **11 Mint Chocolate Chip** Farrow & Ball Vert de Terre 234; Fired Earth Moonstone **12 Chicory Tip** Dulux 50GY 65/084; Flamant 162 Lichen

PAGE 109 APPLE
1 Apple Lime Dulux 34GY 40/515; Crown Paints RAL 6018 **2 Apple Orchard** Crown Paints Caterpillar 12 E 53; Dulux 10GY 41/600 **3 Lime Grass** Dulux 10GY 52/541; Crown Paints Historic Colours H3.29.65 **4 Bramley** Crown Paints Lime Green; Homebase Lime **5 Tasty Apple** Dulux 88YY 66/447; Crown Historic Paints G8.31.76 **6 Green Sherbet** Dulux 10GY 79/231; Homebase Soft Green **7 Emerald** Francesca's Paints Emerald Green; Crown Paints Venetian Green 14 E 51 **8 Jade** Farrow & Ball Arsenic 214; Little Greene Paint Company Green Verditer 92 **9 Mint Julep** Nutshell Natural Paints 123CAS5; Homebase Spearmint **10 Chameleon** Dulux 9GY 76/158; Crown Paints Cool Aqua **11 Celadon** Nutshell Natural Paints 123CAS4; Homebase Meadow **12 Cool Mint** Dulux 09GY 83/104; Crown Paints Dewdrop 14 C 31

PAGE 109 OLIVE
1 Antique Green Little Greene Paint Company Olive Colour 72; Fired Earth Wild Olive 120 **2 Herb Garden** Sanderson Forrest 38-32T; Fired Earth Zangar Green 108 **3 Forest Hills Green** Little Greene Paint Company Garden 86; Flamant 192 Petit Pois **4 Faded Green** Francesca's Paints Casa Bruciata's Muddy Green; Flamant SE309 Pastis **5 Spring Valley** Little Greene Paint Company Paint Company Tracery II; Sanderson Sheer Green 39-19P 78 **6 Fresh Dew** Flamant 171 Thé Vert; Farrow & Ball Green Ground 206 **7 Deep Sea Green** Dulux 30GG 09/106; Farrow & Ball Carriage Green 94 **8 Gothic Green** Farrow & Ball Minster Green 224; Dulux 70GY 14/187 **9 Willow Grove** Francesca's Paints Chiara's Dirty Green; Farrow & Ball Calke Green 34 **10 Winchester Sage** Farrow & Ball Folly Green 76; Francesca's Paints Lucia's Apple Green **11 Meadow** Little Greene Paint Company Pea Green 91; Dulux 70GY 46/120 **12 Dew** Fired Earth Celadon 110; Dulux 70GY 63/098

PAGE 112 FOREST SYMPHONY
1 Sage Green Francesca's Paints Mint III; Fired Earth Summer Lichen 109 **2 Chicory Tip** Dulux 50GY 65/084; Flamant 162 Lichen **3 White Truffle** Dulux 71YY 87/078; Francesca's Paints Boiled Egg I **4 Vienna Green** Dulux 10GY 40/296; Crown Paints Historic Colours H3.29.65 **5 Caribbean Coast** Dulux 74BG 61/206; Crown Paints Blue Note **6 Saffron** Francesca's Paints Arabella's Pumpkin; Dulux 90YR 34/561

PAGE 112 GUSTAVIAN GREEN
1 Mint Chocolate Chip Farrow & Ball Vert de Terre 234; Fired Earth Moonstone **2 Gustavian Green** Francesca's Paints Casa Bruciata's Muddy Green; Crown Paints Peridot 12 B 21 **3 Dark Oak** Crown Historic Paints D6.19.52; Farrow & Ball Ointment Pink 21 **4 Deep Night Blue** Farrow & Ball Drawing Room Blue 25; Dulux 50BB 08/171 **5 Cook's Blue** Farrow & Ball Cook's Blue 237; Dulux 50BB 08/171 **6 Clotted Cream** Dulux 55YY 80/072; Little Greene Paint Company Batsman 73

PAGE 113 FRIED GREEN TOMATOES
1 Sage Green Francesca's Paints Mint III; Fired Earth Summer Lichen 109 **2 Spring Greens** Farrow & Ball Saxon Green 80; Sanderson Willow Vale 39-22M **3 Pelican Grey** Dulux 30BB 62/004; Flamant SE332 Atlantic **4 Mother of Pearl** Paint & Paper Library Sand I; Farrow & Ball James White 2010 **5 Ruby Red** Dulux 16YR 16/594; Little Greene Paint Company Firefly 141 **6 Full Bloom** Dulux 54RR 52/260; Crown Powder Pink 02 C 33

PAGE 116 SAGE HAVEN
1 Mint Julep Nutshell Natural Paints 123CAS5; Homebase Spearmint **2 Emerald** Francesca's Paints Emerald Green; Crown Paints Venetian Green 14 E 51 **3 String** Farrow & Ball String 8; Paint & Paper Library Sand V **4 Dark Beige** Farrow & Ball Cat's Paw 240; Paint & Paper Library Paper V **5 Blazer Red** Farrow & Ball Blazer 212; Dulux 10YR 13/437 **6 Fashion Pink** Dulux 90RR 52/214; Sanderson Sangaree 17-23M

PAGE 117 APPLE DINER
1 Bramley Crown Paints Lime Green; Homebase Lime **2 Midnight Green** Farrow & Ball Minster Green 224; Sanderson Forrest 38-32T **3 Paddington Blue** Dulux 39BB 18/351; Crown Paints RAL 5012 **4 Blue Bayou** Dulux 90BG 50/157; Sanderson Gown Blue 26-22M **5 Natural White** Farrow & Ball Strong White 2001; Flamant 105 Castle Whitel **6 Seed Pod** Farrow & Ball Savage Ground 213; Dulux 20YY 63/149

Page 120 GREEN MIST
1 Faded Green Francesca's Paints Casa Bruciata's Muddy Green; Flamant SE309 Pastis **2 Pine Tree** Farrow & Ball Cooking Apple Green 32; Little Greene Paint Company Kitchen Green 85 **3 Cornforth White** Farrow & Ball Cornforth White; Francesca's Paints The MIST **4 Beige Sand** Farrow & Ball London Stone 6; Sanderson Mushroom Grey Lt. 47-20P **5 Brassy Gold** Dulux 50YY 49/191; Crown Historic Paints G0.26.61 **6 London Burgundy** Dulux 70YR 13/140; Crown Historic Paints C9.08.39

121 CHINESE GREEN
1 Deep Sea Green Dulux 30GG 09/106; Farrow & Ball Carriage Green 94 **2 All White** Farrow & Ball All White 2005; Paint & Paper Library Chaste **3 Willow Grove** Francesca's Paints Chiara's Dirty Green; Farrow & Ball Calke Green 34 **4 Miami Teal** Dulux 50GG 50/320; Little Greene Paint Company Turquoise Blue 93 **5 Dinky Pink** Farrow & Ball Middleton Pink 245; Paint & Paper Library Coral 1 **6 Claret Rose** Dulux 30YR 15/550; Crown Paints Geranium 04 E 53

PAGE 121 MOROCCAN MIX
1 Forest Hills Green Little Greene Paint Company Garden 86; Flamant 192 Petit Pois **2 Strong Red** Farrow & Ball Rectory Red 217; Dulux 05YR 15/555 **3 Summer Straw** Farrow & Ball Hay 37; Little Greene Paint Company Chamois 132 **4 Great Green** Farrow & Ball Green Ground 206; Little Greene Paint Company Eau de Nil 90 **5 Pulsating Blue** Dulux 98BG 26/393; Homebase Cobalt **6 Buttercup Yellow** Farrow & Ball Babouche 223; Little Greene Paint Company Light Gold 53

EARTH & CLAY

PAGE 125
Mud Flat Farrow & Ball Dutch Pink 62; Dulux 00YY 43/304 **Brown Sugar** Farrow & Ball India Yellow 66; Little Greene Paint Company Light Buff 45 **Mocha Express** Crown Historic Paints C9.0839; Flamant 153 Potatoes **Texas Rose** Farrow & Ball Porphry Pink 49; Dulux 10YR 22/206 **Beige Sand** Farrow & Ball London Stone 6; Sanderson Mushroom Grey **Sable Fur** Little Greene Paint Company Paint Company Roman Plaster 31; Crown Paints Picnic Basket **Cracked Wheat** Farrow & Ball Mouse's Back 40; Flamant 178 Peanuts **Milk Chocolate** Flamant P38 Sienna; Paint & Paper Library Hot Earth

PAGE 128 CINNAMON
1 Santa Fe Dulux 10YY 27/600; Crown Paints Bokhara 06 D 43 **2 Allspice** Farrow & Ball Sand; Dulux 00YY 28/352 **3 Brown Sugar** Farrow & Ball India Yellow 66 ; Little Greene Paint Company Light Buff 45 **4 Mud Flat** Farrow & Ball Dutch Pink 62; Dulux 00YY 43/304 **5 Ochre** Little Greene Paint Company Straw Colour 44; Nutshell Natural Paints 107CA55 **6 Oklahoma Wheat** Paint & Paper Library Whitington; Dulux 20YY 67/216 **7 Burnt Sienna** Little Greene Middle Buff 122; Dulux 00YY 26/520 **8 Orange Tan** Paint & Paper Library The Long Room; Homebase Soft Terracotta **9 Saffron** Francesca's Paints Arabella's Pumpkin; Dulux 90YR 34/561**10 Beeswax** Francesca's Paints Watago Sand; Dulux 90YR 49/382 **11 Acorn** Farrow & Ball Orangery 70; Dulux 10YY 45/419 **12 Ashbury Sand** Little Greene Paint Company Cream Colour 55; Dulux 10YY 65/285

PAGE 128 ADOBE
1 Milk Chocolate Flamant P38 Sienna; Paint & Paper Library Hot Earth **2 Noisette** Dulux 70YR 35/216; Paint & Paper Library Tudor Rose **3 Mink** Little Greene Paint Company Button 27; Flamant P33 Terre de Picardie **4 Putty** Farrow & Ball Setting Plaster 231; Crown Historic Colours E1.11.67 **5 Milk Shake** Paint & Paper Library Wild Silk; Crown Paints Walnut **6 Pumice** Paint & Paper Library Coral II; Crown Paints Coral Pink 04 E 49 **7 Oxblood** Dulux 23YR 08/237; Flamant P41 Monseigneur **8 Boston Brick** Dulux 10YR 17/184; Little Greene Paint Company Ashes of Roses 4 **9 Texas Rose** Farrow & Ball Porphry Pink 49; Dulux 10YR 22/206 **10 Polished Plaster** Dulux 10YR 37/143; Flamant 180 Vintage **11 Pueblo** Flamant 181 Blush; Dulux 10YR 67/111 **12 Fairest Pink** Dulux 50YR 76/087; Crown Historic Paints E5.05.81

PAGE 129 MOLE
1 Taupetone Dulux 80YR 27/147; Crown Paints Brown Sugar **2 Woodacres** Dulux 90YR 26/147; Fired Earth Raw Earth 17 **3 Sable Fur** Little Greene Paint Company Roman Plaster 31; Crown Paints Picnic Basket **4 Tupelo Taupe** Dulux 40YR 43/101; Farrow & Ball Dead Salmon 28 **5 Beige Sand** Farrow & Ball London Stone 6; Sanderson Mushroom Grey Lt. 47-20P **6 Chalk Pit** Dulux 30YY 60/104; Farrow & Ball Skimming Stone 241**7 Brownstone** Dulux 10YY 14/080; Fired Earth Antique Earth 24 **8 Café Crème** Dulux 20YY 22/129; Flamant P15 Gris Souris **9 Raccoon Hollow** Dulux 20YY 31/106; Flamant SE 324 Flax **10 Brandon Beige** Dulux 40YY 38/107; Fired Earth Oak Apple 9 **11 French Linen** Dulux 50YY 57/082; Flamant PO2 Craic **12 Tapestry Beige** Dulux 40YY 67/087; Flamant SE335 Weekend

PAGE 129 CHOCOLATE
1 Cup O'Java Paint & Paper Library Hopsack; Little Greene Paint Company Felt 145 **2 Saddle Brown** Dulux 70YR 11/279; Francesca's Paints The EARTH **3 Savannah** Dulux 80YR16/193; Homebase Delicious; **4 Bitter Chocolate** Dulux 70YR 18/184; Crown Historic Paints C8.16.45 **5 Dark Oak** Crown Historic Paints D6.19.52; Farrow & Ball Ointment Pink 21 **6 Nutmeg** Paint & Paper Library Roben's Honour; Little Greene Paint Company Tuscany 12 **7 Mahogany** Farrow & Ball London Clay 244; Little Greene Paint Company Attic II **8 Mocha Express** Crown Historic Paints C9.0839; Flamant 153 Potatoes **9 Truffle** Dulux 80Y 17/129; Sanderson Arroyo Brown 52-6D **10 Cracked Wheat** Farrow & Ball Mouse's Back 40; Flamant 178 Peanuts **11 Smooth Pebble** Farrow & Ball Dauphin 54; Paint & Paper Library Moth **12 Camel's Back** Paint & Paper Library Sand III; Farrow & Ball Off-White 3

PAGE 132 ISLAND SPICE
1 Brown Sugar Farrow & Ball India Yellow 66 ; Little Greene Paint Company Ligh **2 Beige Sand** Farrow & Ball London Stone 6; Sanderson Mushroom Grey Lt. 47-20P **3 Golden Yellow** Dulux 23YY 61/631; Crown Historic Paints F3.40.76 **4 Mandarin Fruit** Dulux 80YR 37/516; Crown Paints Tango 06 E 51 **5 Grey Suede** Farrow & Ball Charleston Gray 243; Fired Earth Amber Gris 30 **6 Leather** Dulux 70YR 16/345; Crown Paints Caramel 06 C 37

PAGE 133 FEELING THE HEAT
1 Acorn Farrow & Ball Orangery 70; Dulux 10YY 45/419 **2 Orange Tan** Paint & Paper Library The Long Room; Homebase Soft Terracotta **3 Clover White** Little Greene Paint Company Rusling 9; Dulux 00YY 83/069 **4 Red Rock** Dulux 10YR 15/500; Crown Historic Paints B8.33.45 **5 Chilli Pepper** Dulux 16YR 16/594; Little Greene Paint Company Firefly **6 Jet Night** Farrow & Ball Mahogany 36 Crown Historic Paints TN.02.24

PAGE 133 BATHED IN SPICE
1 Texas Rose Farrow & Ball Porphry Pink 49; Dulux 10YR 22/206 **2 Tapestry Beige** Dulux 40YY 67/087; Flamant SE335 Weekend **3 Cotton Ball** Farrow & Ball Blackened 2011; Dulux 70YY 72/041 **4 Meadowlands Green** Dulux 90GY 47/328; Crown Paints Venetian Green 14 E 51 **5 Racing Green** Dulux 90GY 13/375; Crown Paints RAL 6001 **6 Olympus Green** Dulux 90GG 08/118; Crown Beetle Green 14 C 39

PAGE 136 TREETOP COOL
1 Noisette Dulux 70YR 35/216; Paint & Paper Library Tudor Rose **2 Putty** Farrow & Ball Setting Plaster 231; Crown Historic Colours E1.11.67 **3 Willow Grove** Francesca's Paints Chiara's Dirty Green; Farrow & Ball Calke Green 34 **4 Orbit Glow** Francesca's Paints Barbara's Pink; Little Greene Paint Company Orange Aurora 21 **5 Hot Red** Farrow & Ball Blazer 212; Sanderson Cardinal Red 17-28T **6 Vineyard** Farrow & Ball Pelt 254; Sanderson Bitter Plum 20-28T

PAGE 137 MUD, GLORIOUS MUD
1 Milk Chocolate Flamant P38 Sienna; Paint & Paper Library Hot Earth **2 Pumice** Paint & Paper Library Coral II; Crown Paints Coral Pink 04 E 49 **3 All White** Farrow & Ball All White 2005; Little Greene Paint Company Shirting 129 **4 Hadley Red** Little Greene Paint Company Adventurer 7; Farrow & Ball Brinjal 222 **5 Monticello Rose** Farrow & Ball Setting Plaster 231; Crown Historic Paints D0.07.69 **6 Toasted Bean** Dulux 70YR 09/086; Little Greene Paint Company Squash Brown 32

PAGE 140 SILVER GREY
1 Tupelo Taupe Dulux 40YR 43/101; Farrow & Ball Dead Salmon 28 **2 Shadow Grey** Fired Earth Oak Apple 9; Sanderson Westminster 47-11M **3 Cloudy Grey** Dulux 71YY 87/078; Francesca's Paints Boiled Egg I **4 Cotton Ball** Farrow & Ball Blackened 2011; Dulux 70YY 72/041 **5 Grass** Dulux 30GY51/294; Fired Earth Absinthe 112 **6 Jungle** Dulux 90BG 10/067; Farrow & Ball Black Blue 95

PAGE 141 FIRED EARTH
1 Sable Fur Little Greene Paint Company Roman Plaster 31; Crown Paints Picnic Basket **2 Flax** Dulux 40YY 67/087; Flamant SE335 Weekend **3 Savoury Cream** Little Greene Paint Company Co Old Paper II 146; Nutshell Natural Paints 126ECO3 **4 Pumpkin Spice** Dulux 80YR 34/468; Francesca's Paints Sienna **5 Shy Cherry** Dulux 10YR 15/500; Little Greene Paint Company Drummond 16 **6 Misty Morning** Dulux 30BB 62/044; Fired Earth Pearl Ashes 3

PAGE 144 TOPAZ & TOFFEE
1 Mahogany Farrow & Ball London Clay 244; Little Greene Paint Company Attic II **2 Salsa** Farrow & Ball Cochineal 65; Dulux 16YR 16/594 **3 Café Latte** Dulux 30YY 65/171; Little Greene Paint Company Pitcairn 61 **4 Glimmer** Dulux 45YY 69/614; Francesca's Paints Yellow Peppers **5 Citronee** Farrow & Ball White Tie 2002; Little Greene Paint Company Linnet 89 **6 Seaport Blue** Dulux 10BB 12/310; Crown Historic Paints R5.28.43

PAGE 145 MOCHA LIVING
1 Cup O'Java Paint & Paper Library Hopsack; Little Greene Paint Company Felt 145 **2 Saddle Brown** Dulux 70YR 11/279; Francesca's Paints The EARTH **3 Forest Green** Farrow & Ball Calke Green 34; Dulux 70GY 27/154 **4 Antique Brown** Farrow & Ball Buff 20; Little Greene Paint Company Stone-Dark-Warm 36 **5 Deep Gilt** Farrow & Ball India Yellow 66; Sanderson Spice Tan 5-18D **6 Mouse Grey** Farrow & Ball Light Blue 22; Homebase Silver Mist

NIGHT & DAY

PAGE 149
Stainless Steel Dulux 30BG 72/017; Farrow & Ball Skylight 205 **Snow White** Dulux 30GY 88/014; Crown Historic Paints G8.03.88 **Pewter** Crown Historic Paints RN.02.70; Dulux 30BB 53/012 **Blackboard** Dulux 90BG 16/060; Crown Historic Paints T1.04.40 **Airforce Blue** Crown Historic Paints RO.04.39; Homebase Slate **White Ice** Dulux 30GY 83/043; Little Greene Paint Company Starling's Egg 97

PAGE 152 SNOW
1 Nautical White Farrow & Ball Lime White 1; Homebase Putty **2 Arctic Fox** Paint & Paper Library Marble I; Sanderson Ice Cascade 44-2P **3 China Cup** Farrow & Ball Slipper Satin 2004; Little Greene Paint Company Stock 37 **4 Egyptian Cotton** Paint & Paper Library Sand III; Crown Historic Paints G3.08.83 **5 Chalk** Francesca's Paints White Truffle; Sanderson Grey Birch Lt. 47-2P **6 Mother of Pearl** Paint & Paper Library Sand I; Farrow & Ball James White 2010 **7 White Ice** Dulux 30GY 83/043; Little Greene Paint Company Starling's Egg 97 **8 Polar Bear** Dulux 30GY 83/021; Francesca's Paints Pool of Shahdarat **9 Tundra Ice** Fired Earth Bianco; Little Greene Paint Company Clock Face 81 **10 Winter Snow** Fired Earth Bianco; Little Greene Paint Company Clock Face 81 **11 Titanium White** Dulux 98YY 82/022; Francesca's Paints Emperor's Marble **12 Snow White** Dulux 30GY 88/014; Crown Historic Paints G8.03.88

PAGE 152 METALLIC GREY
1 Grey Mountain Little Greene Paint Company Dark Lead Colour 118; Crown Historic Paints VN.02.36 **2 Sterling Silver** Dulux 50YR 38/017; Little Greene Paint Company Lead Colour 117 **3 Dove** Dulux 50YR 45/014; Farrow & Ball Lamp Room Gray 242 **4 Pearl** Dulux 50YR 62/008; Farrow & Ball Pavilion Gray 242 **5 Silver Birch** Dulux 00YY 63/024; Little Greene Paint Company Welcome 109 **6 Chrome** Dulux 80 YR 83/017; Little Greene Paint Company China Clay 1 **7 Blackboard** Dulux 90BG 16/060; Crown Historic Paints T1.04.40 **8 Bachelor Blue** Dulux 90BG 25/079; Fired Earth Plumbago 5; Little Greene Paint Company Juniper Ash 115 **9 Black Ash** Dulux 90BG 41/040; Little Greene Paint Company James 108 **10 Gustavian Grey** Dulux 90BG 48/057; Farrow & Ball Parma Gray 27 **11 Gunmetal** Dulux 50BG 64/028; Francesca's Paints Hibiscus Blue **12 Stainless Steel** Dulux 30BG 72/017; Farrow & Ball Skylight 205

PAGE 153 SLATE
1 Charcoal Farrow & Ball Railings 31; Dulux 50BG 08/021 **2 Deep Slate** Farrow & Ball Down Pipe 26; Sanderson Black Pearl 44-6D **3 Graphite** Dulux 30BB 31/043;Little Greene Mid Lead Colour 114 **4 Elephant Grey** Dulux 90BG 41/040; Crown Historic Paints 58.04.55 **5 Pewter** Crown Historic Paints RN.02.70; Dulux 30BB 53/012 **6 Pelican Grey** Dulux 30BB 62/004; Flamant SE332 Atlantic **7 Squid Ink** Dulux 90BG 08/075; Farrow & Ball Off-Black 57 **8 Airforce Blue** Crown Historic Paints RO.04.39; Homebase Slate **9 Bluff Cove** Little Greene Paint Company Bone China Blue 107; Homebase Dove Grey **10 Silver Mink** Farrow & Ball Light Blue 22; Homebase Silver Mist **11 Ice Blue** Farrow & Ball Borrowed Light 235; Dulux 50GG 63/042 **12 Grey Ash** Dulux 50GG 73/031; Little Greene Paint Company Echo 98

PAGE 156 LOFTY WHITES
1 Jute Dulux 30GY 83/043; Little Greene Paint Company Starling's Egg 97 **2 Charcoal** Farrow & Ball Railings 31; Dulux 50BG 08/021 **3 Forest Hills Green** Little Greene Paint Company Garden 86; Flamant 192 Petit Pois **4 Turkish Coffee** Dulux 30YY 11/076; Farrow & Ball London lay 244 **5 Bronzed Brown** Farrow & Ball Dauphin 54; Little Greene Paint Company Silt 40 **6 Walled Garden** Farrow & Ball Calke Green 34; Dulux 50GY 18/178

PAGE 157 WHITE WOOD
1 Mother of Pearl Paint & Paper Library Sand I; Farrow & Ball James White 2010 **2 Pale Pear** Dulux 30GY 83/107; Crown Historic Colours J0.08.80 **3 Yukon Sky** Dulux 70BB 49/082; Crown Historic Paints V8.003.56 **4 Tupelo Green** Fired Earth Celadon 110; Sanderson Will-o'-the-Wisp 34-7P **5 Cayman Blue** Dulux 50BG 41/312; Homebase Azure **6 Passion Plum** Dulux 73RB 08/259; Crown Paints Emperor 24 C 39

PAGE 161 DECO SHIMMER
1 Dove Dulux 50YR 45/014; Farrow & Ball Lamp Room Gray 242 **2 Bluff Cove** Little Greene Paint Company Bone China Blue 107; Homebase Dove Grey **3 Dark Walnut** Dulux 30YR 07/157; Sanderson Bitter Plum 20-28T **4 Velvety Red** Dulux 50RR 11/286; Fired Earth Surpar Red 71 **5 Green Horizon** Fired Earth Northern Lights 98; Sanderson Airlane Blue 28-13P **6 Green Hint** Fired Earth Moonstone 103; Crown Historic Paints K1.03.81

PAGE 161 PEWTER PERFECTION
1 Gustavian Grey Dulux 90BG 48/057; Farrow & Ball Parma Gray 27 **2 Stainless Steel** Dulux 30BG 72/017; Farrow & Ball Skylight 205 **3 Darkest Grape** Dulux 90BB 19/165; Fired Earth Amethyst 83 **4 Antique Lace** Dulux 40YY 79/168; Sanderson Metropolitan Lt.7-14P **5 Natural Canvas** Dulux 30YY 78/018; Farrow & Ball Strong White 2001 **6 Smoky Blue** Dulux 10BB 57/115; Homebase Iris

PAGE 164 TROPICAL GLAMOUR
1 Graphite Dulux 30BB 31/043;Little Greene Paint Company Mid Lead Colour 114 **2 Pelican Grey** Dulux 30BB 62/004; Flamant SE332 Atlantic **3 Cotton Ball** Farrow & Ball Blackened 2011; Dulux 70YY 72/041 **4 Cabernet** Dulux 50RB 13/107; Fired Earth Amethyst 83 **5 Witching Hour** Flamant P96 Black Tie; Crown Historic Paints TN.02.24 **6 Province Blue** Dulux 50BG 32/114; Crown Historic Paints Q0.07.56

PAGE 164 BLACK NOTES
1 Pelican Grey Dulux 30BB 62/004; Flamant SE332 Atlantic **2 Silver Mink** Farrow & Ball Light Blue 22; Homebase Silver Mist **3 Chrome** Dulux 80 YR 83/017; Little Greene Paint Company China Clay 1 **4 Marble Canyon** Fired Earth Malm 35; Crown Historic Paints F8.06.73 **5 Potters Clay** Dulux 80YR 26/323; Crown Historic Paints D6.19.52 **6 Deep Indigo** Dulux 00NN 13/000; Little Greene Paint Company Jet Black 119

PAGE 165 FINE DINING
1 Charcoal Farrow & Ball Railings 31; Dulux 50BG 08/021 **2 Lantern Light** Fired Earth Light Gamboge 51; Little Greene Paint Company Stargazer 68 **3 Clotted Cream** Dulux 55YY 80/072; Little Greene Paint Company Batsman 73 **4 Deep Ocean Blue** Dulux 70BG 09/171; Flamant P94 Blue Jeans **5 Hollow Brown** Dulux 80YR 27/147; Crown Historic Paints C8.16.45 **6 Moleskin** Little Greene Paint Company Stone-Dark-Cool 67; Dulux 30YY 44/114

Page 166 NORTHERN LIGHTS
1 Airforce Blue Crown Historic Paints RO.04.39; Homebase Slate **2 Pewter** Crown Historic Paints RN.02.70; Dulux 30BB 53/012 **3 Titanium White** Dulux 98YY 82/022; Francesca's Paints Emperor's Marble **4 Georgian Green** Farrow & Ball Lichen; Flamant P69 Lake Green **5 Richmond Gold** Dulux 90YR 33/167; Fired Earth Palm Honey 48 **6 Smooth Pebble** Sanderson Westminster 47-11M; Crown Historic Paints F4.07.63

PAGE 166 TOTAL TAR
1 Charcoal Farrow & Ball Railings 31; Dulux 50BG 08/021 **2 White Ice** Dulux 30GY 83/043; Little Greene Paint Company Starling's Egg 97 **3 Elephant Grey** Dulux 90BG 41/040; Crown Historic Paints 58.04.55 **4 Midnight Navy** Dulux 70BG 07/086; Sanderson Skipper Blue 26-32T **5 Dove** Dulux 50YR 45/014; Farrow & Ball Lamp Room Gray 242 **6 Grey Shingle** Farrow & Ball Hardwick White 5; Fired Earth Oak Apple 9

PAGE 167 GREEN & BLACK
1 Charcoal Farrow & Ball Railings 31; Dulux 50BG 08/021 **2 Pelican Grey** Dulux 30BB 62/004; Flamant SE332 Atlantic **3 Snow White** Dulux 30GY 88/014; Crown Historic Paints G8.03.88 **4 Fairmont Green** Fired Earth Zangar Green 108; Farrow & Ball Calke Green 34 **5 Salisbury Green** Sanderson Driftwood Grey 42-15P; Flamant 162 Lichen **6 Bright and Early** Flamant 169 Angel; Homebase Waterfall

PAGE 167 SAFARI PLAINS
1 Airforce Blue Crown Historic Paints RO.04.39; Homebase Slate **2 Ochre** Little Greene Paint Company Straw Colour 44; Nutshell Natural Paints 107CA55 **3 Mother of Pearl** Paint & Paper Library Sand I; Farrow & Ball James White 2010 **4 Galveston Grey** Farrow & Ball Lamp Room Grey 88; Flamant P28 Zinc **5 Roxbury Caramel** Farrow & Ball Dutch Pink 62; Flamant P34 Dalle Industrielle **6 Shaker Beige** Dulux 20YY 57/178; Francesca's Paints Gianluca's Fawn

PANNACOTTA & CAPPUCCINO

PAGE 171
Alabaster Crown Paints Moonlight 18 C 31; Francesca's Paints Pavilion **Natural Canvas** Dulux 30YY 78/018; Farrow & Ball Strong White 2001 **Butter Churn** Fired Earth Marble 43; Dulux 20YY 83/063 **Café Latte** Dulux 30YY 65/171; Little Greene Pitcairn 61 **Lily of the Valley** Dulux 42YY 87/084; Francesca's Paints Sand I **Bleached Beech** Dulux 40YY 72/164; Francesca's Paints Moonlight

PAGE 174 RICOTTA
1 Cotton Ball Farrow & Ball Blackened 2011; Dulux 70YY 72/041 **2 Orchid** Dulux 70YY 73/083; Francesca's Paints Truffle **3 Clotted Cream** Dulux 55YY 80/072; Little Greene Paint Company Batsman 73 **4 Mother of Pearl** Paint & Paper Library Sand I; Farrow & Ball James White 2010 **5 Alabaster** Crown Paints Moonlight 18 C 31; Francesca's Paints Pavilion **6 Calla Lily** Crown Paints Peppermint; Francesca's Paints Mint II **7Jute** Dulux 30YY 78/035; Little Greene Paint Company Joanna 130 **8 String** Dulux 30YY 69/048; Little Greene Paint Company Mirage II **9 Oatmeal** Dulux 50YY 63/041; Francesca's Paints Mist; Little Greene Paint Company Welcome 109 **10 Natural Canvas** Dulux 30YY 78/018; Farrow & Ball Strong White 2001 JL2 **11 Bone** Dulux 70YY 72/041; Little Greene Paint Company Linen Wash 33 **12 Mimosa** Dulux OONN 83/000; Francesca's Paints Emperor's Marble

PAGE 174 BUTTERMILK
1 Papyrus Little Greene Paint Company Magnolia 28; Farrow & Ball Ringwold Ground 208 **2 Curd** Little Greene Paint Company Old Paper II 146; Farrow Ball New White 59 **3 Cow's Milk** Dulux 44YY 70/112; Francesca's Paints Atone **4 Popcorn** Dulux 44YY 80/106; Francesca's Paint Christophe's White **5 Lily of the Valley** Dulux 42YY 87/084; Francesca's Paints Sand I **6 Vanilla** Dulux 40YY 83/086; Farrow & Ball White Tie 2002 **7 Crème Brûlée** Dulux OOYY 76/088; Farrow & Ball Pink Ground 202 **8 Sesame Seed** Little Greene Paint Company Inner Shell II; Dulux 10YY 76/104 **9 Salmon White** Dulux 90YR 77/115 ; Paint & Paper Library Coral **10 Clover White** Benjamin Moore Ambrosia 893; Sherwin-Williams 6323 Romance **11 Warm Blush** Fired Earth White Mezereon 74; Sanderson Congo Pink 10-19P **12 Butter Churn** Fired Earth Marble 43; Dulux 20YY 83/063

PAGE 175 BISCOTTI
1 Barley Dulux 60YY 77/180; Francesca's Paint Boiled Egg II **2 Natural Calico** Dulux 45YY 76/146; Francesca's Paint Cream **3 Shortbread** Dulux 40YY 79/168; Francesca's Paints Mascarpone **4 Cornish Cream** Dulux 45YY 77/183; Farrow & Ball House White 2012 **5 White Truffle** Dulux 71YY 87/078; Francesca's Paints Boiled Egg **6 Dairy Milk** Dulux 60YY 83/094; Francesca's Paints Poppy Cream **7 Parchment** Little Greene Paint Company Clay 39; Paint & Paper Library Paper IV **8 Café Latte** Dulux 30YY 65/171; Little Greene Paint Company Pitcairn 61 **9 Cashmere** Dulux 40YY 72/164; Farrow & Ball String 8 **10 Bleached Beech** Dulux 40YY 72/164; Francesca's Paints Moonlight**11 Oat Cake** Dulux 30YY 62/127; Paint & Paper Library Suede III **12 Limewash** Dulux 44YY 70/110; Paint & Paper Library Suede 1

PAGE 178 SPRING COLOURS
1 Clotted Cream Dulux 55YY 80/072; Little Greene Paint Company Batsman 73 **2 Chalk Pit** Dulux 30YY 60/104; Farrow & Ball Skimming Stone 241**3 Pewter** Crown Historic Paints RN.02.70; Dulux 30BB 53/012 **4 Yellow Flower** Dulux 50YY 71/369; Crown Historic Paints F8.25.79 **5 Billowy Down** Dulux 50BG 74/130; Crown Historic Paints M5.04.80 **6 Cactus Flower** Dulux 90RR 21/418; Crown Historic Paints B4.27.45

PAGE 179 LILAC LINEN
1 Alabaster Crown Paints Moonlight 18 C 31; Francesca's Paints Pavilion **2 Clotted Cream** Dulux 55YY 80/072; Little Greene Paint Company Batsman 73 **3 Beige Sand** Farrow & Ball London Stone 6; Sanderson Mushroom Grey Lt. 47-20P **4 Lavender Blue** Dulux 10 RB 35/167; Crown Paints Purple Rain **5 Wild Orchid** Dulux 50RB 34/153; Crown Historic Paints V8.03.56 **6 Exotic Red** Dulux 00YR 15/510; Homebase Cherry

PAGE 182 STRAWBERRIES & CREAM
1 Curd Little Greene Paint Company Old Paper II 146; Farrow Ball New White 59 **2 Winter Snow** Crown Paints A Whisper of Mellow Sage; Paint & Paper Library Marble 1 **3 Dark Oak** Crown Historic Paints D6.19.52; Farrow & Ball Ointment Pink 21 **4 Deep Rose** Paint & Paper Library Beetlenut; Dulux 10YR 13/437 **5 Mauve Mist** Dulux 10YR 37/143; Paint & Paper Library Diva **6 Mauve Sable** Francesca's Paints Mud; Crown Historic Paints C8.16.45

PAGE 183 BUTTERCUP & MOLE
1 Lily of the Valley Dulux 42YY 87/084; Francesca's Paints Sand I **2 Stoneground** Dulux 45YY 67/259; Farrow & Ball Farrow's Cream 67 **3 Allspice** Farrow & Ball Sand; Dulux 00YY 28/352 **4 Blueberry** Dulux 10BB 12/310; Crown Paints RAL 5017 **5 Paper White** Little Greene Paint Company Linen Wash 33; Francesca's Paint French Grey **6 French Horn** Francesca's Paints Mud; Paint & Paper Library Snettisham Gold

PAGE 186 CAPPUCCINO SCREEN
1 Parchment Little Greene Paint Company Clay 39; Paint & Paper Library Paper IV **2 Golden Wheat** Farrow & Ball Cat's Paw 240; Paint & Paper Library Chalk V **3 Green Pearl** Sanderson Ice Cascade 44-1P; Flamant P171 The Vert **4 Field Green** Dulux 30GG 16/137; Crown Historic Paints L9.12.51 **5 Mocha Express** Crown Historic Paints C9.0839; Flamant 153 Potatoes **6 Pale Primrose** Francesca's Paints Boiled Egg III; Dulux 53YY 83/348

PAGE 187 FADE TO GREY
1 White Truffle Dulux 71YY 87/078; Francesca's Paints Boiled Egg I **2 Cornish Cream** Dulux 45YY 77/183; Farrow & Ball House White 2012 **3 Barley** Dulux 60YY 77/180; Francesca's Paint Boiled Egg II **4 Mauve Sand** Benjamin Moore Hint of Violet 2114-60; Sherwin-Williams 6051 Sashay Sand **5 Espresso Bean** Benjamin Moore Desert Shadows 2114-30; Sherwin-Williams 6006 Black Bean **6 Purple Taupe** Benjamin Moore Wet Concrete 2114-40; Sherwin-Williams 7509 Tiki Hut

Page 187 FIELDS OF BARLEY
1 Bleached Beech Dulux 40YY 72/164; Francesca's Paints Moonlight **2 Parchment** Little Greene Paint Company Clay 39; Paint & Paper Library Paper IV **3 Ochre** Little Greene Paigt Company Straw Colour 44; Nutshell Natural Paints 107CA55 **4 Popcorn** Dulux 44YY 80/106; Francesca's Paint Christophe's White **5 Winchester Sage** Farrow & Ball Folly Green 76; Francesca's Paints Lucia's Apple Green **6 Caramel Latte** Farrow & Ball Straw 52; Crown Historic Paints E7.17.65

Suppliers

ARCHITECTS AND DESIGNERS

1100 Architect
New York, USA
Tel:+ 1 212 645 1011
www.1100architect.com

Atelier Abigail Ahern
London, UK
+44(0) 20 7354 8181
www.atelierabigailahern.com

Abraham & Thakore Ltd
New Delhi, India
Tel: + 91 11 699 3714
www.abrahamandthakore.com

Karim el Achak Architects
Marrakesh, Morocco
Tel:+ 212 24 44 73 13

Jenny Armit
London Tel: + 44 (0) 20 7792 2121
Los Angeles Tel: + 1 310 659 5261
www.jennyarmit.com

Paolo Badesco
Milan, Italy
Tel: + 39 (0) 24 100737
www.paolobadesco.it

Linda Barker
London, UK
Tel: +44 845 330 2880
www.reallylindabarker.co.uk

John Barman
New York, USA
Tel: + 1 212 838 9443
www.johnbarman.com

Atlanta Bartlett
Kent, UK
Tel: + 44 (0) 1797 344 077
www.paleandinteresting.com

Solis Betancourt
Washington, D.C. USA
Tel: + 1 202 659 8734
www.solisbetancourt.com

Jeffrey Bilhuber
Bilhuber & Associates
New York, USA
Tel: + 1 212 308 4888
www.bilhuber.com

Sonja and John Caproni
Caproni Associates, New York, USA
Tel:+ 1 212 977 4010

Alexandra Champalimaud & Associates
New York, USA
Tel: + 1 212 807 8869
www.alexchamp.com

Don Chapell (Deceased)
Guy Peterson/Ofa
Sarasota, Florida, USA
Tel:+ 1 941 952 1111
www.guypeterson.com

Jane Churchill
London, UK
Tel: +44 (0) 20 7244 7427
www.janechurchill.com

Clodagh Design
New York, USA
Tel: + 1 212 780 5755
www.clodagh.com

David Collins Architecture and Design
London, UK
Tel: + 44 (0) 20 7835 5000
www.davidcollins.com

Coorengel & Calvagrac
Paris, France
Tel:+ 33 1 40 27 14 65
www.coorengel-calvagrac.com

Agnès Comar
Paris, France
Tel:+ 33 1 47 23 33 85

Bernie de Le Cuona
London, UK
Tel: +44 (0) 20 7584 7677
www.delecuona.co.uk

Jamie Drake
New York, USA
Tel:+ 1 212 754 3099
www.drakedesignassociates.com

Agnès Emery
Brussels Tel:+ 32 2 513 5892
London Tel: c/o Retrouvius + 44 (0) 20 8969 0222
www.emeryetcie.com

Luigi Esposito
London, UK
Tel: +44 (2) 20 7584 9495
www.casaforma.co.uk

Ramón Esteve Architects
Valencia, Spain
Tel:+ 34 96 351 04 34
www.ramonesteve.com

Frank Faulkner
Catskill, New York, USA
Tel: + 1 518 943 9220
www.frankfaulkner.com

Patrizio Fradiani
Studio F, Chicago, Illinois, USA
Tel:+ 1 773 880 0450
www.studiof-design.com

Anne Fougeron
San Francisco, CA, USA
Tel: + 1 415 641 5744
www.fougeron.com

Karl Fournier and Olivier Marty
Studio KO, Paris, France &
Marrakesh, Morocco
Paris Tel:+ 33 1 42 71 13 92
www.studioko.fr

Christophe Gollut
London, UK
Tel: +44 20 7370 4021

Philip Gorrivan Design
New York, USA
Tel: +1 212 339 7696
www.philipgorrivan.com

Johnny Grey
Hampshire, UK
Tel: + 44 (0) 1730 821424
Mount Clemens, Michigan, USA:
Tel:+ 1 888 902 8860
www.johnnygrey.com

John Hobby
Space, Atlanta, Georgia
Tel: + 1 404 228 4600
www.spacemodern.com

Dominique Kieffer
Paris Tel:+ 33 1 56 81 20 20
London Tel: + 44 (0)20 7349 1590
www.dkieffer.com

Hilton McConnico
Bagnolet, France
Tel: + 33 143 625 316
www.hiltonmcconnico.com

Ilaria Miani
Rome, Italy
Tel:+ 39 06 6833160
www.ilariamiani.it

John Minshaw Designs Ltd
London, UK
Tel: + 44 (0) 20 7486 5777
www.johnminshawdesigns.com

Mimmi O'Connell
London, UK
Tel: +44 (0) 20 7752 0474
www.mimmioconnell.com

John Pardey Architects
Hampshire, UK
Tel: + 44 (0) 1590 626465
www.johnpardeyarchitects.com

Paul + O Architects
London, UK
Tel: + 44 (0) 20 7604 3818
www.paul-o-architects.com

Lena Proudlock
Denim in Style, Tetbury, UK
Tel: + 44 (0) 1666 50051
www.lenaproudlock.com

Karim Rashid
New York, USA
Tel: + 1 212 929 8656
www.karimrashid.com

Jonathan Reed
Studio Reed, London, UK
Tel: + 44 (0) 20 7565 0066

Johann Slee
Stellenbosch, South Africa
Tel:+ 27 21 887 3385
www.slee.co.za

Rupert Spira
UK
Tel: + 44 (0) 1588 650588
www.rupertspira.com

Philippe Stark
Paris, France
Tel:+ 33 1 48 07 54 54
www.stark.com

John Stefanidis
London, UK
Tel: + 44 2(0) 7808 4700
www.johnstefanidis.com

Axel Vervoordt
Gravenwezel, Belgium
Tel: + 32 658 1470
www.axel-vervoordt.com

Nicolas Vignot
Paris, France
Tel: + 33 6 11 96 67 69
http://n.vignot.free.fr

Peter Wadley Architects
London, UK
Tel: + 44 (0) 20 8747 8833
www.wadleyarchitects.com

John Wardle Architects
Melbourne, Victoria, Australia
Tel: + 61 39 6548700
www.johnwardle.com

Donald A. Wexler Associates
California, USA
Tel: + 1 760 320 1709

SHOPS

ABC Carpet & Home
New York, USA
Tel: + 1 212 473 3000
www.abchome.com

GP & J Baker
London, UK
Tel: + 44 (0) 20 7351 7760
www.gpjbaker.com

Solgården
Stockholm, Sweden
Tel:+ 46 8 663 9360
www.solgarden.net

Traditions
New York, USA
Tel:+ 1 518 851 3975

PAINT SUPPLIERS

Auro Natural Paints
Cheltenham Road
Bisley, Nr Stroud
Gloucestershire GL6 7BX, UK
Tel: +44 (0) 1452 772020
www.auro.co.uk

Behr Paints
3400 W Segerstrom Ave
Santa Ana, CA 92704, USA
Tel: + 1 714 545 7101
www.behr.com

Benjamin Moore & Co
101 Paragon Drive
Montvale, NJ 07645, USA
Tel: + 1 800 344 0400
www.benjaminmoore.com

Calico Corners
Customer Service, 203 Gale Lane
Kennett Square, PA 19348, USA
Tel: + 1 800 213 6366
www.calicocorners.com

Craig & Rose
Unit 8, Halbeath Industrial Estate,
Dunfermline, Fife KY11 7EG, UK
Tel: + 44 (0) 1254 704951
www.craigandrose.com

Crown Paints
Hollins Road
Darwen BB3 OBG, UK
Tel: + 44 (0) 870 240 1127
www.crownpaint.co.uk

Dulux Paints
Slough, UK
Tel: + 44 (0) 870 444 11 11
www.dulux.co.uk

Ecos Organic Paints
Unit 19, Heysham Business Park
Middleton Road, Heysham
Lancs LA3 3PP, UK
Tel: + 44 (0) 1524 852371
www.ecospaints.com

Farrow & Ball
Uddens Estate, Wimborne
Dorset BH21 7NL, UK
Tel: +44 (0) 1202 876141
www.farrow-ball.com

Fine Paints of Europe
P O Box 419
Woodstock, VT 05091, USA
Tel: + 1 800 332 1556
www.finepaintsofeurope.com

Fired Earth Interiors
3 Twyford Mill, Oxford Road,
Adderbury, Nr Banbury,
Oxfordshire OX17 3SX, UK
Tel: + 1 1295 812088
www.firedearth.com

Flamant
The Original Paint Collection
p/a Dendermondsesteenweg 75
B-9300 Aalst, Belgium
Tel: +32 (0) 53 76 80 21
www.flamantpaint.com

Francesca's Paints
Unit 34, Battersea Business Centre
99/109 Lavender Hill
London SW11 5QL, UK
Tel: + 44 (0) 20 7228 7694
www.francescaspaint.com

The Freshaire Choice Paints
Tel: + 1 866 880 0304
www.thefreshairechoice@ici.com
No-VOC paint from ICI available at Home Depot

Glidden
ICI Paints
Cleveland, Ohio, USA
Tel: + 1 800 454 3336
www.glidden.com

Home Depot
Tel: +1 800 553 3199
www.homedepot.com

Kelly Hoppen Interiors
2 Munden Street
London W14 ORH, UK
Tel: + 44 (0) 20 747 3350
www.kellyhoppen.com

ICI Paints
Slough, UK
Tel: + 44 (0) 870 444 11 11
www.dulux.co.uk

Ralph Lauren Paint
Tel: + 1 800 379 POLO
www.ralphlaurenhome.com

Leyland Paints
Tel: +44 (0) 1924 354600
www.leyland-paints.co.uk

The Little Greene Paint Company
Wood Street, Openshaw,
Manchester M11 2FB, UK
Tel: +44 (0) 161 2300 880
www.thelittlegreene.com

Marston & Langinger
192 Ebury Street
London SW1W 8UP, UK
Tel: +44 (0) 20 7881 5710
www.marston-and-langinger.com

Nordic Style
109 Lots Road, London SW10 020
Tel: + 44 (0) 20 7451 1753
www.nordicstyle.biz

Nutshell Natural Paints
Unit 3, Leigham Units
Silverton Road, Matford Park
Exeter, Devon, EX2 8HY, UK
Tel: + 44 (0) 1392 823760
www.nutshellpaints.com

Old Village Paint
P O Box 130
Perkiomenville, PA 18074, USA
Tel: + 1 800 498 7687
www.old-village.com

The Paint & Paper Library
5 Elystan Street
London SW3 3NT, UK
Tel: + 44 (0) 20 7823 7755
www.paintlibrary.co.uk

Papers and Paints
4 Park Walk
London SW10 0AD, UK
Tel: + 44 (0) 20 7352 8626
www.papers-paints.co.uk

Plascon Paints
South Africa
Tel: + 27 (0) 860 204060
www.plascon.co.za

Porter's Paints
895 Bourke St
Waterloo, Sydney
NSW 2017, Australia
www.porterspaints.com.au
Tel: + 61 (0) 2 9698 5322

Restoration Hardware
2900 North MacArthur Drive
Suite 100
Tracy, CA 95376
Tel: +1 800 910 9836
www.restorationhardware.com

Sherwin-Williams
Tel: +1 800 832 2541
www.sherwin-williams.com

Annie Sloan Paints
117 London Road, Headington
Oxford, Oxon OX3 9HZ, UK
Tel: + 44 (0) 1865 768666
www.anniesloan.com

Martha Stewart Colours
Tel: + 1 888 562 7842
www.marthastewart.com
Available only at Lowe's USA

Sun Wallpaper & Paint
47 Overocker Road
Poughkeepsie, NY 12603, USA
Tel: + 1 845 471 2880
www.sunwallpaperandpaint.com

Acknowledgements

No book of this sort could ever achieve perfection without the assistance of many specialist paint producers, colour experts and designers. Once again I find I have had the very generous assistance of many friends and colleagues who have given their valuable time to guide me through the maze of colour available to us today.

Francesca Wezel – my friend, colleague and valued advisor – once again stepped in and talked me through every colour under the sun with her usual vigour, excitement, talent and inspiration. Whether she was explaining to me how bathrooms should always be painted pink as it is the most flattering colour, or helping me find the perfect off-white, she never lost patience or originality. Nor did she ever make me feel I was a nuisance – and I am sure I was. An enormous thank you to Francesca on my behalf and on yours, too, dear reader!

Thank you, David Oliver, for teaching us how to see the colour on different sides of the room by using a shoe box. Thank you Luigi Esposito, Vicente Wolf, Jamie Drake and Agnès Emery for your professional secrets on creating wonderful living spaces – all different and all fascinating.

Kit Kemp, legendary hotel designer, gave us hints as to the use of colour that must appeal to multiple people.

Alex Bates, the Creative Director of West Elm, gave us wonderful colour advice, both personal and professional, for which I am so grateful.

Picture credits

Every effort has been made to trace the copyright holders, architects and designers. We apologize in advance for any unintentional omission and would be pleased to insert the appropriate acknowledgment in any subsequent edition.

Location/Designer or Architect (stylist)/Photographer/Agency

1 Andrea Gobbi/Simon Upton/The Interior Archive, **2** Paolo Badesco's villa in Italy/Andrew Wood, **4** Abraham & Thakore/Andrew Wood, **6** an apartment in Paris, designed by Hilton McConnico/Simon Upton, **9 above left** The Hotelito in Mexico/Jenny Armit/Simon Upton; **9 above right** a house in Marrakesh, designed by Karl Fournier and Olivier Marty/Studio KO/Andrew Wood, **9 below right** Ulla Hagar Tornos/Fritz von der Schulenburg/The Interior Archive, **9 below left** Lena Proudlock of Denim In Style's house in Gloucestershire/Simon Upton, **12 above** Jamie Drake/Fritz von der Schulenburg, **12 below** a house in Marrakesh, designed by Karl Fournier and Olivier Marty/Studio KO/Andrew Wood, **13 above left** Jane Churchill/Simon Upton, **13 above right** Simon Upton, **13 below right** Shane/Cooper Residence in New York/1100 Architects/Andrew Wood, **13 below left** Jane Churchill/Simon Upton, **14 above left** a house in Balnarring in Coastal Victoria/John Wardle Architects/Andrew Wood, **14 above right** Denis Blais (Vingt Douze)/Luke White/The Interior Archive. **15 left** Susanne Boyd/Simon Upton/The Interior Archive, **15 right** Jane Churchill/Simon Upton, **16 above left** Hilton McConnico's house in Paris/Simon Upton, **16 above right** Jamie Drake's apartment in New York/Andrew Wood, **16 below right** Philip Gorrivan/Simon Upton/The Interior Archive, **16 below left** Johnny Grey/Alex Wilson, **17** Jane Churchill/Simon Upton, **18 left** Linda Barker/Lucinda Symons, **18 right** a house in the Hamptons, designed by Solis Betancourt/Simon Upton, **19** Linda Barker/Lucinda Symons, **25 above left** The Hotelito in Mexico/Jenny Armit/Simon Upton, **25 above right** Philippe Stark/Simon Upton/The Interior Archive, **25 below right** Eric and Gloria Stewart's manor house in southwestern France /Simon Upton, **25 below left** Peter Wadley/Tim Beddow/The Interior Archive, **26** Ilaria Miani/Simon Upton, **28** Jane Churchill/Simon Upton, **29** Armand Ventilo/Mark Luscombe-Whyte/The Interior Archive, **30 left** Jane Churchill/Simon Upton, **30 right** Linda Barker/Lucinda Symons, **31** Jane Churchill/Simon Upton, **32** Richard Mudditt/Fritz von der Schulenburg/The Interior Archive, **33** Jane Churchill/Simon Upton, **34** Jane Churchill/Simon Upton, **35** Mary Drysdale's house in Pennsylvania/Andrew Wood, **36** John Stefanidis/Fritz von der Schulenburg/The Interior Archive, **37** Manolo Mestre/Mark Luscombe-Whyte/The Interior Archive, **38** Jamie Drake/Fritz von der Schulenburg, **39** Alex Possenbacher/Mark Luscombe-Whyte/The Interior Archive, **45 above left** Rupert Spira/Simon Upton, **45 above right** Karim Rashid/Andrew Wood, **45 below** The Hotelito in Mexico/Jenny Armit/Simon Upton, **46** Jane Churchill/Simon Upton, **48** Ali Sharland's house in Gloucestershire/Simon Upton, **49** Shane/Cooper Residence in New York/1100 Architects/Andrew Wood, **50** Christophe Gollut's house in Gran Canaria/Simon Upton, **51** Agnès Comar/Fritz von der Schulenburg, **52** John Pardey/Mark Luscombe-Whyte/The Interior Archive, **53** Andrew Allfree/Simon Upton/The Interior Archive, **54** Designer: Jim Isermann; Architect: Donald Wexler/Mark Luscombe-Whyte/The Interior Archive, **55** Francoise Smilenko/Vincent Knapp/The Interior Archive, **56** Charles de Sellier's house in Brussels/Simon Upton, **57** Lincoln/Orum Residence in Suffolk/Angi Lincoln/Andrew Wood, **58** Abraham & Thakore/Andrew Wood, **59 left** Karim el Achak's house in Marrakesh/Andrew Wood, **59 right** Karim el Achak's house in Marrakesh/Andrew Wood, **65 above left** Luke White, **65 above right** The Hotelito in Mexico/Jenny Armit/Simon Upton, **65 below** Jenny Armit/Simon Upton, **67** Michael Coorengel & Jean-Pierre Calvagrac/Fritz von der Schulenberg, **68** Nicholas Alvis Vega and Liza Bruce/Simon Upton/The Interior Archive, **69** an apartment in Paris, designed by Hilton McConnico/Simon Upton, **70 left** Fishman Residence in Florida/Don Chapell/Andrew Wood, **70 right** Lynne Fornieles of Febo Design/Andrew Wood, **71** Fishman Residence in Florida/Don Chapell/Andrew Wood, **72** Nathalie Lete/Frederic Vasseur/The Interior Archive, **73-74** Jenny Armit/Simon Upton, **75** Jamie Drake's apartment in New York/Simon Upton, **76** Nathalie Lete/Frederic Vasseur/The Interior Archive, **77** Karim el Achak's house in Marrackech/Andrew Wood, **78** Michael Coorengel & Jean-Pierre Calvagrac/Fritz von der Schulenberg, **79** Nathalie Lete/Frederic Vasseur/The Interior Archive, **85 above left** Fishman Residence in Florida/Don Chapell/Andrew Wood, **85 above right** Agnès Emery's house in Marrakesh/Simon Upton, **85 below right** Andrea Gobbi/Simon Upton/The Interior Archive, **85 below left** Carlos Mota (Miles Redd)/Simon Upton/The Interior

Archive, **86** Jane Churchill/Simon Upton, **88** Jane Churchill/Simon Upton, **89** Hilton McConnico/Simon Upton, **90 left** Graham Head (of ABC Carpet & Home) and Barbara Rathbourne's house in Long Island/Andrew Wood, **90 right** Barbara Kurgan and James Andrew/Simon Upton/The Interior Archive, **91** Jane Churchill/Simon Upton, **92** Jane Churchill/Simon Upton, **93** Jane Churchill/Simon Upton, **94** Neilama Residence, Helsinki/Ulla Koskinen/Andrew Wood, **95** Agnès Emery's house in Marrakesh/Simon Upton, **96** a house in Ibiza, designed by Ramón Esteve Architects/Andrew Wood, **97** Linda Barker/Lucinda Symons, **98** John Minshaw Designs Ltd/Simon Upton/The Interior Archive, **99** a riverside apartment in London, designed by Luigi Esposito/Luke White, **100** Elena and Stephen Georgiadis' house in London/John Minshaw Designs Ltd/Simon Upton, **101 left** Agnès Emery's house in Marrakesh/Simon Upton, **101 right** Axel Vervoordt's house in Belgium/Simon Upton, **107 above left** Agnès Emery's house in Marrakesh/Simon Upton, **107 above right** Penny Morrison/Tim Beddow/The Interior Archive, **107 below** Paul + O Architects/Mark Luscombe-Whyte/The Interior Archive, **108** Julie Prisca's house in Normandy/Simon Upton, **110** George Residence, extension and remodelling/Michael George/Andrew Wood, **111** Jane Churchill/Simon Upton, **112 left** Lynn von Kersting/Andrew Wood, **112 right** Peri Wolfman and Charles Gold's house in Bridgehampton/Simon Upton, **113** Jane Churchill/Simon Upton, **114** Pamela Kline (of Traditions)'s house in Claverack, New York/Simon Upton, **115** Jane Churchill/Simon Upton, **116** Jane Churchill/Simon Upton, **117** Mark Luscombe-Whyte/The Interior Archive, **118** a house in Connecticut, designed by Jeffrey Bilhuber/Simon Upton, **119** Shane/Cooper Residence in New York/1100 Architects/Andrew Wood, **120** David Collins Architecture and Design/Fritz von der Schulenberg, **121 left** David Carter/Simon Upton, **121 right** Nathan Turner/Simon Upton, **127 above left** Codman House, a property of the Society of the Preservation of New England Antiquities/Simon Upton, **127 above right** a house in Marrakesh designed by Karl Fournier and Olivier Marty/Studio KO/Andrew Wood, **127 below right** Bernie de la Cuona/Simon Upton, **127 below left** a house in London, designed by Jonathan Reed/Simon Upton, **130** Carlos Mota and Miles Redd/Simon Upton/The Interior Archive, **131** Jamie Drake/Fritz von der Schulenberg, **132** a penthouse in New York, designed by Clodagh Design/Luke White, **133 left** Andrew Wood **133 right** Ianthe Ruthven/The Interior Archive, **134 & 135** a house in Marrakesh, designed by Karl Fournier & Olivier Marty/Studio KO/Andrew Wood, **136 & 137** Johann Slee's house in Johannesburg/Andrew Wood, **138** Jeffrey Bilhuber/Simon Upton, **139** Virginia Fisher/Fritz von Schulenburg/The Interior Archive, **140** a house in London by Jonathan Reed/Simon Upton, **141** an apartment in Paris, designed by Hilton McConnico/Simon Upton, **142** Bernie de Le Cuona/Luke White, **143** Ilaria Miani/Simon Upton, **144** Philip Gorrivan/Simon Upton/The Interior Archive, **145** Patrick Gwynne/Tim Beddow/the Interior Archive, **151 above left** Axel Vervoordt/Simon Upton, **151 above right** Véronique Lopez's house from Casa Lopez/Simon Upton, **151 below right** Linda Barker(Towbridge Prints)/Lucinda Symons, **151 below left** Dominique Kieffer's house in Normandy/Simon Upton, **153** Mimmi O'Connell/Simon Upton, **154** Jane Churchill/Simon Upton, **155** Mark Gilbey and Polly Dicken's house in Pennsylvannia/Simon Upton, **156** Vincente Wolf/Andrew Wood, **157** Jane Churchill/Simon Upton, **158** Michael Coorengel & Jean-Pierre Calvagrac's apartment in Paris/Luke White, **159–160** Linda Barker (Crown Paint)/Lucinda Symons, **161** Marianne von Kantzow's shop Solgården in Stockholm/Simon Upton, **162** Dominique Kieffer's house in Normandy/Simon Upton, **163** John Barman's apartment in New York/Simon Upton, **164 left** Paolo Badesco's villa in Italy/Andrew Wood, **164 right** Frank Faulkner's house in Catskill, New York/Simon Upton, **165** Alexandra Champalimaud/Simon Upton, **166 left** Peri Wolfman and Charles Gold's house in Bridgehampton/Simon Upton, **166 right** Dominique Kieffer's house in Normandy/Simon Upton, **167 left** Kristiina Ratia's house in Connecticut/Andrew Wood, **167 right** Jeffrey Bilhuber/Simon Upton, **173 above left** Mannisto/Poyhonen apartment in Helsinki/Tuula Poyhonen/Andrew Wood, **173 above right** Jeannette Chang's apartment in New York/Sonja & John Caproni/Simon Upton, **173 below right** a house in Atlanta designed by Tim Hobby of Space/Simon Upton, **173 below left** a house in Connecticut designed by Jeffrey Bilhuber/Simon Upton, **175** Jane Churchill/Simon Upton, **176** Dominique Kieffer's house in Normandy/Simon Upton, **177** Patrizio Fradiani's house in Chicago/Patrizio Fradiani at Studio F/Frederic Vasseur, **178** Graham Head (of ABC Carpet & Home) and Barbara Rathbourne's house in Long Island/Andrew Wood, **179** Jane Churchill/Simon Upton, **180** Andrew Wood, **181-183** Jane Churchill/Simon Upton, **184** Anthony Cochrane's apartment in New York/Simon Upton, **185** Jane Churchhill/Simon Upton, **186** Matthew Drennan and Hamish McArdle's house in London/Dalsouple/Lucinda Symons, **187 left** a riverside apartment in London designed by Luigi Esposito/Luke White, **187 right** Jane Churchill/Simon Upton